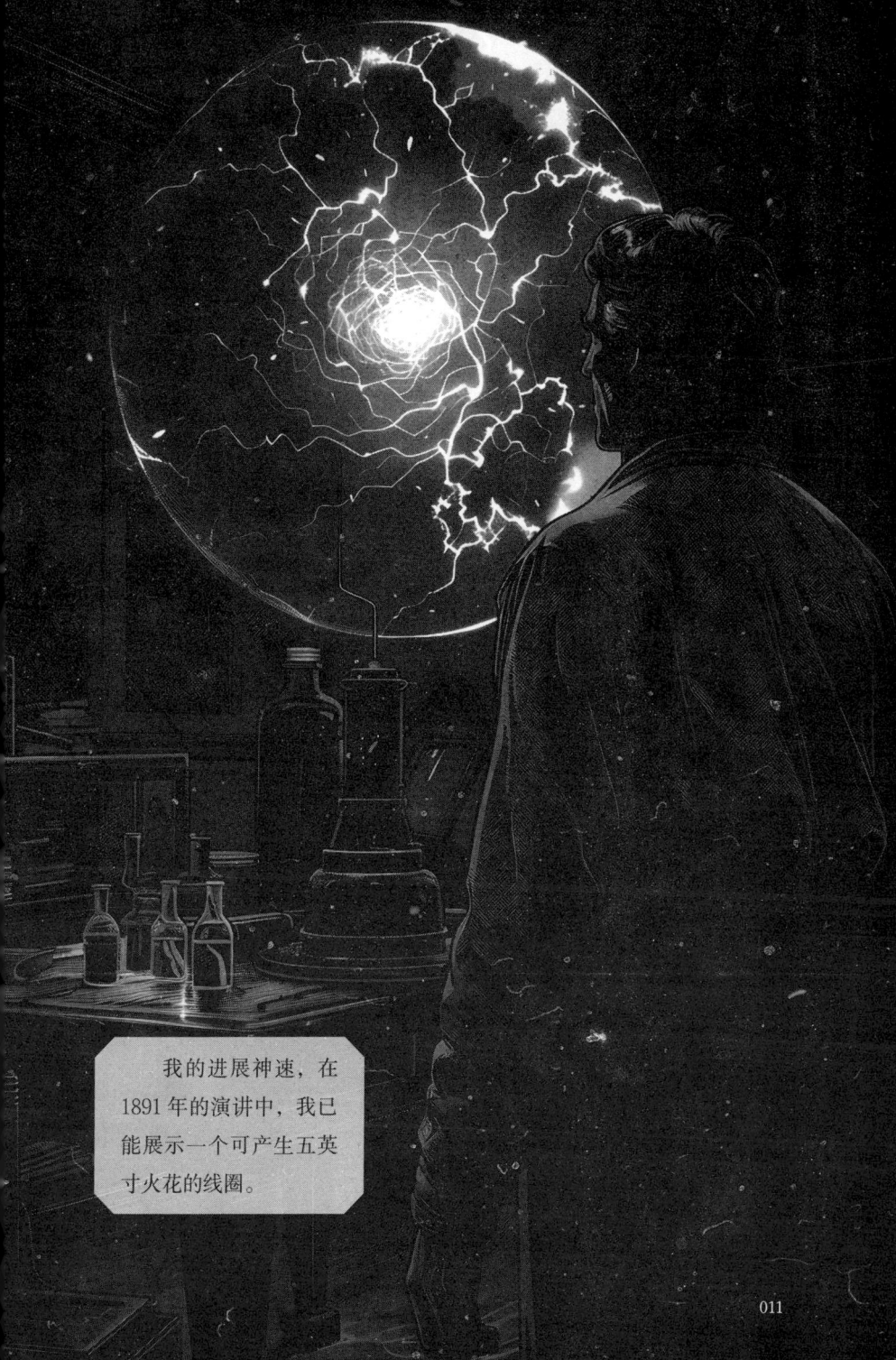

我的进展神速,在1891年的演讲中,我已能展示一个可产生五英寸火花的线圈。

之前在研究高频电流时,我惊喜地发现,在一定空间里可以产生足够强度的电场来点亮无电极真空管。

众所周知,大气层中的电流和机器产生的电流是完全一样的。很显然,自然电流和人造电流的干扰也以完全相同的方式在地面和空中传播,并且在水平和垂直两个方向上都产生了电动势。

特斯拉自传

[美] 尼古拉·特斯拉 著
张文明 译

Nikola Tesla

民主与建设出版社
·北京·

©民主与建设出版社，2024

图书在版编目（CIP）数据

特斯拉自传 /（美）尼古拉·特斯拉著；张文明译. -- 北京：民主与建设出版社，2024.4
ISBN 978-7-5139-4565-3

Ⅰ.①特… Ⅱ.①尼… ②张… Ⅲ.①特斯拉（Tesla, Nikola 1856-1943）-自传 Ⅳ.①K837.126.1

中国国家版本馆CIP数据核字（2024）第092333号

特斯拉自传
TESILA ZIZHUAN

著　　者	［美］尼古拉·特斯拉
译　　者	张文明
责任编辑	宁莲佳
特约策划	任程民
封面设计	王娇娇
出版发行	民主与建设出版社有限责任公司
电　　话	（010）59417747　59419778
社　　址	北京市海淀区西三环中路10号望海楼E座7层
邮　　编	100142
印　　刷	三河市骏杰印刷有限公司
版　　次	2024年4月第1版
印　　次	2024年6月第1次印刷
开　　本	880毫米×1230毫米　1/32
印　　张	7.5
字　　数	119千字
书　　号	ISBN 978-7-5139-4565-3
定　　价	49.80元

注：如有印、装质量问题，请与出版社联系。

目 录

Ⅰ. My Early Life
第一章　我的早年 ································· 1

Ⅱ. My First Efforts in Invention
第二章　发明初体验 ······························ 35

Ⅲ. My Later Endeavors
第三章　后期诸尝试 ······························ 67

Ⅳ. The Discovery of the Tesla Coil and Transformer
第四章　特斯拉线圈和变压器的发现 ············ 99

Ⅴ. The Magnifying Transmitter
第五章　放大发射器 ····························· 127

Ⅵ. The Art of Telautomatics
第六章　遥控力学的艺术 ························ 163

译者后记 ·· 218

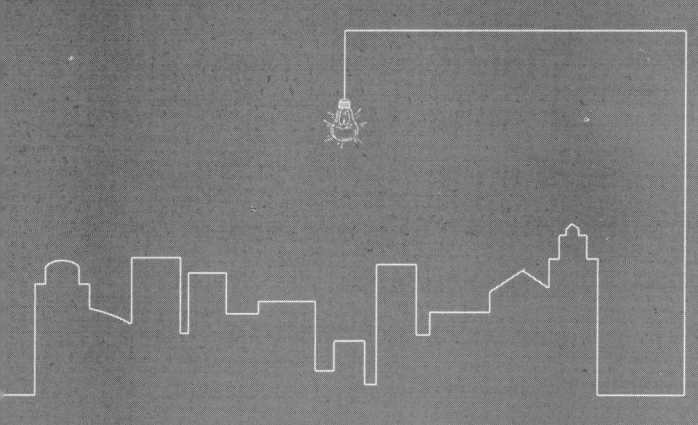

I . My Early Life
第一章 我的早年

The progressive development of man is vitally dependent on invention. It is the most important product of his creative brain. Its ultimate purpose is the complete mastery of mind over the material world, the harnessing of the forces of nature to human needs. This is the difficult task of the inventor who is often misunderstood and unrewarded. But he finds ample compensation in the pleasing exercises of his powers and in the knowledge of being one of that exceptionally privileged class without whom the race would have long ago perished in the bitter struggle against pitiless elements.

Speaking for myself, I have already had more than my full measure of this exquisite enjoyment, so much that for many years my life was little short of continuous rapture. I am credited with being one of the hardest workers and perhaps I am, if thought is the equivalent of labor, for I have devoted to it almost all of my waking hours. But if work is interpreted to be a definite performance in a specified time according to a rigid rule, then I may be the worst of idlers. Every effort under compulsion demands a sacrifice of life-energy. I never paid such a price. On the contrary, I have thrived on my thoughts.

In attempting to give a connected and faithful account of my activities in this series of articles which will be presented with the assistance of the Editors of the ELECTRICAL EXPERIMENTER and

第一章 我的早年
I . My Early Life

人类的不断进步主要依赖于发明。作为人类大脑创造力最重要的产物,发明的最终目的是以思想之力掌控物质世界,驭自然之力满足人类需求。这项艰巨任务落到了发明家肩上,而他们却常常被误解,甚至被埋没。但是,发明家们仍醉心发明,乐此不疲。作为一个特殊的群体,要不是他们,人类也许早就在与冷酷自然的激烈对抗中消亡了。

就我本人而言,我已充分体会到了这份极致的愉悦。多年来,我的生活从来不缺狂喜。有人说我是工作狂,如果思考也是一种工作的话,或许我的确是,因为我几乎把我所有清醒的时间都花在了思考上。但是,如果工作被解释为在特定时间内按照严格的规则完成一定的业绩,那么我可能是最糟糕的懒汉。任何被迫而为的事都是在消耗生命的能量,所幸我从不曾这样。恰恰相反,我因思考而茁壮成长。

尽管很不情愿,但在《电气实验者》编辑们的协助下,我还是撰写了一系列面向青少年读者的文章,其中包括我的一些真实经历,详细地记述了我青少年时代的记忆以及那些决定我

are chiefly addrest to our young men readers, I must dwell, however reluctantly, on the impressions of my youth and the circumstances and events which have been instrumental in determining my career.

Our first endeavors are purely instinctive, promptings of an imagination vivid and undisciplined. As we grow older reason asserts itself and we become more and more systematic and designing. But those early impulses, although not immediately productive, are of the greatest moment and may shape our very destinies. Indeed, I feel now that had I understood and cultivated instead of suppressing them, I would have added substantial value to my bequest to the world. But not until I had attained manhood did I realize that I was an inventor.

This was due to a number of causes. In the first place I had a brother who was gifted to an extraordinary degree—one of those rare phenomena of mentality which biological investigation has failed to explain. His premature death left my parents disconsolate. We owned a horse which had been presented to us by a dear friend. It was a magnificent animal of Arabian breed, possessed of almost human intelligence, and was cared for and petted by the whole family, having on one occasion saved my father's life under remarkable circumstances. My father had been called one winter night to perform an urgent duty and while crossing the mountains, infested by wolves, the horse became

第一章 我的早年
Ⅰ. My Early Life

发明生涯的往事。

年幼时，我们努力纯粹是出自本能，受驱于鲜活而又不受约束的想象力。随着年龄的增长，理性开始发挥作用，我们变得越来越有条理，思维也越来越清晰。早年间的那些冲动，虽没有立即产生效用，却是决定我们命运最关键的瞬间。事实上，我现在觉得，如果当初我懂得这一点并去浇灌而不是压制冲动，我留给世界的财富一定会更有价值。但直到成年后，我才意识到我是一个发明家。

这有多方面的因素。我曾有一个哥哥，他天资卓越，智力超群，罕见到从生物学角度都无法解释的地步。他的早逝让我的父母悲痛欲绝。我们有一匹马，是一位好朋友送给我们的。那是一匹阿拉伯良种马，十分通人性，全家人对它疼爱有加，它曾在危急关头救过我父亲的命。那是一个冬夜，父亲奉命去执行一项紧急任务，在穿越山区时，这匹马受惊于狼群骚扰，失控而逃，将父亲重重摔在地上。到家的时候，它浑身是血，精疲力竭，但是嘶鸣示警后，又立即冲了出去，回到了出事地点。搜救队伍没走多远，就遇到了骑着马的父亲，他已经恢复了知觉，并没有意识到自己已经在雪地里躺了几个小时。我的

frightened and ran away, throwing him violently to the ground. It arrived home bleeding and exhausted, but after the alarm was sounded immediately dashed off again, returning to the spot, and before the searching party were far on the way they were met by my father, who had recovered consciousness and remounted, not realizing that he had been lying in the snow for several hours. This horse was responsible for my brother's injuries from which he died. I witnessed the tragic scene and although fifty-six years have elapsed since, my visual impression of it has lost none of its force. The recollection of his attainments made every effort of mine seem dull in comparison.

Anything I did that was creditable merely caused my parents to feel their loss more keenly. So I grew up with little confidence in myself. But I was far from being considered a stupid boy, if I am to judge from an incident of which I have still a strong remembrance. One day the Aldermen were passing through a street where I was at play with other boys. The oldest of these venerable gentlemen—a wealthy citizen—paused to give a silver piece to each of us. Coming to me he suddenly stopped and commanded, "Look in my eyes." I met his gaze, my hand outstretched to receive the much valued coin, when, to my dismay, he said, "No, not much, you can get nothing from me, you are too smart." They used to tell a funny story about me. I had two old aunts with wrinkled faces, one of them having two teeth protruding like the tusks

哥哥就是因为这匹马而受伤,最后不幸离世的。我亲眼看到了那悲惨的一幕,尽管已经过去56年,仍历历在目。回忆起哥哥的成就,我的每一次努力都显得黯淡无光,不值一提。

我所做的任何值得称赞的事,都只会加深父母的丧子之痛,所以我从小就对自己缺乏信心。但我也绝非一个笨小孩,这点从一件我至今仍记忆犹新的事上可以得到验证。有一天,市议员们经过一条街道,我正和其他男孩在那里玩耍。这些德高望重的绅士中最年长的一位——一个有钱人——停下来给我们每人一枚银币。他朝我走来,突然停住,命令道:"看着我的眼睛。"我迎上他的目光,伸手去接那枚价值不菲的硬币,他却说:"不,你从我这儿什么也得不到,你太聪明了。"他们还讲过另一件关于我的趣事。我有两个阿姨,她们都上了年纪,满脸皱纹,其中一个长有两颗龅牙,如同象牙一般,每次她亲我的时候那两颗牙都很扎脸。没有什么比被这些既热情又不漂亮

of an elephant which she buried in my cheek every time she kissed me. Nothing would scare me more than the prospect of being hugged by these as affectionate as unattractive relatives. It happened that while being carried in my mother's arms they asked me who was the prettier of the two. After examining their faces intently, I answered thoughtfully, pointing to one of them, "This here is not as ugly as the other."

Then again, I was intended from my very birth for the clerical profession and this thought constantly oppressed me. I longed to be an engineer but my father was inflexible. He was the son of an officer who served in the army of the Great Napoleon and, in common with his brother, professor of mathematics in a prominent institution, had received a military education but, singularly enough, later embraced the clergy in which vocation he achieved eminence. He was a very erudite man, a veritable natural philosopher, poet and writer and his sermons were said to be as eloquent as those of Abraham a Sancta-Clara. He had a prodigious memory and frequently recited at length from works in several languages. He often remarked playfully that if some of the classics were lost he could restore them. His style of writing was much admired. He penned sentences short and terse and was full of wit and satire. The humorous remarks he made were always peculiar and characteristic. Just to illustrate, I may mention one or two instances. Among the help there was a cross-eyed man called Mane, employed

的亲戚拥抱更让我害怕的了。有一次，母亲抱着我，碰巧有人问我这两个人中谁更漂亮。端详了她们的脸后，我若有所思地指着其中一位说道："这个阿姨没有那个丑。"

话又说回来，我从一出生就注定要继承父业，从事神职人员的工作，这件事一直困扰着我。我渴望成为一名工程师，但我的父亲却固执己见。我的祖父是一名军官，曾在拿破仑的军队中服役。我有一个叔叔，是一所著名高校的数学教授，他们都曾接受过军事教育，但奇怪的是，我父亲后来投身于神职事业，并在这个行业中声名显赫。他是一个非常博学的人，是一位名副其实的哲学家、诗人和作家，据说他的布道和亚伯拉罕·阿·圣克塔·克拉拉（Abraham a Sancta-Clara）的一样精彩。他记忆力惊人，经常用好几种语言大段背诵各种经典。他常开玩笑说，如果一些经典作品失传了，他可以还原。他的文风备受推崇，句子短小精悍，亦庄亦谐。他的幽默言论总是独具特色。为了说明这一点，我可以举一两个例子。有一个名叫马尼（Mane）的斗鸡眼男人，受雇在农场干活。一天，他正在砍柴。当他抡起斧头时，我父亲站在旁边感到非常不舒服，就劝他说："看在上帝的分上，马尼，不要砍你盯着的，去砍你想

to do work around the farm. He was chopping wood one day. As he swung the axe my father, who stood nearby and felt very uncomfortable, cautioned him, "For God's sake, Mane, do not strike at what you are looking but at what you intend to hit." On another occasion he was taking out for a drive a friend who carelessly permitted his costly fur coat to rub on the carriage wheel. My father reminded him of it saying, "Pull in your coat, you are ruining my tire." He had the odd habit of talking to himself and would often carry on an animated conversation and indulge in heated argument, changing the tone of his voice. A casual listener might have sworn that several people were in the room.

Although I must trace to my mother's influence whatever inventiveness I possess, the training he gave me must have been helpful. It comprised all sorts of exercises—as, guessing one another's thoughts, discovering the defects of some form or expression, repeating long sentences or performing mental calculations. These daily lessons were intended to strengthen memory and reason and especially to develop the critical sense, and were undoubtedly very beneficial.

My mother descended from one of the oldest families in the country and a line of inventors. Both her father and grandfather originated numerous implements for household, agricultural and other uses. She was a truly great woman, of rare skill, courage and fortitude,

砍的。"还有一次,他驾车带一位朋友去兜风,朋友不小心将自己昂贵的毛皮大衣蹭到了车轮上。我父亲提醒他说:"收起你的大衣,别把我轮胎蹭坏了。"他有自言自语的怪癖,经常会对着空气说话,并沉浸在激烈的争论中,不时改变自己的语音。不仔细听,你肯定会以为房间里有好几个人。

虽然我所拥有的创造力得益于我的母亲,但父亲给我的训练肯定也是有帮助的,他让我做各种练习——揣测他人的想法,发现某种表达的缺陷,复述长句或进行心算。这些日常训练旨在加强记忆和推理能力,特别是在培养批判意识方面,无疑是非常有益的。

我的母亲来自一个发明世家,也是这个国家最古老的家族之一的后裔。她的父亲和祖父都发明了许多家用、农用和其他用途的工具。她是一位真正伟大的女性,拥有罕见的技能、勇气和毅力;她勇敢地面对生活中的风暴,经历过许多艰难的时

who had braved the storms of life and past through many a trying experience. When she was sixteen a virulent pestilence swept the country. Her father was called away to administer the last sacraments to the dying and during his absence she went alone to the assistance of a neighboring family who were stricken by the dread disease. All of the members, five in number, succumbed in rapid succession. She bathed, clothed and laid out the bodies, decorating them with flowers according to the custom of the country and when her father returned he found everything ready for a Christian burial. My mother was an inventor of the first order and would, I believe, have achieved great things had she not been so remote from modern life and its multifold opportunities. She invented and constructed all kinds of tools and devices and wove the finest designs from thread which was spun by her. She even planted the seeds, raised the plants and separated the fibers herself. She worked indefatigably, from break of day till late at night, and most of the wearing apparel and furnishings of the home was the product of her hands. When she was past sixty, her fingers were still nimble enough to tie three knots in an eyelash.

There was another and still more important reason for my late awakening. In my boyhood I suffered from a peculiar affliction due to the appearance of images, often accompanied by strong flashes of light, which marred the sight of real objects and interfered with my

第一章 我的早年
I . My Early Life

刻。在她 16 岁时，一场致命的瘟疫席卷全国。她的父亲被叫去给垂死之人做临终圣礼，在父亲不在的时候，她独自去照顾感染了可怕瘟疫的邻居。邻居家五口人，很快相继死亡。她为他们沐浴更衣，安置遗体，按照当地的习俗用鲜花装饰，当她父亲回来时，发现一切都准备妥当，可以举行基督教葬礼了。我的母亲也是一位一流的发明家。我相信，如果她不是远离现代生活以及缺少机会，她会取得巨大的成就。她发明并制造了各种工具和设备，用她自己纺的线织出了最精美的图案。她甚至自己播种、栽培并分离纤维。她不辞劳苦地工作，从破晓到深夜，家里几乎所有的服饰和装饰都出自她手。她年过六旬时，手指仍然灵活，眨眼间就能打三个结。

我之所以晚熟还有一个更重要的原因。年少时，我得了一种怪病，眼前会出现幻象，还经常伴有强烈的闪光，这种病破坏了我对真实物体的感知，干扰了我的思想和行动。要知道，这些幻象都跟我之前确实见过的物体和事件相关，而不是我凭

thought and action. They were pictures of things and scenes which I had really seen, never of those I imagined. When a word was spoken to me the image of the object it designated would present itself vividly to my vision and sometimes I was quite unable to distinguish whether what I saw was tangible or not. This caused me great discomfort and anxiety. None of the students of psychology or physiology whom I have consulted could ever explain satisfactorily these phenomena. They seem to have been unique although I was probably predisposed as I know that my brother experienced a similar trouble. The theory I have formulated is that the images were the result of a reflex action from the brain on the retina under great excitation. They certainly were not hallucinations such as are produced in diseased and anguished minds, for in other respects I was normal and composed. To give an idea of my distress, suppose that I had witnest a funeral or some such nerve-racking spectacle. Then, inevitably, in the stillness of night, a vivid picture of the scene would thrust itself before my eyes and persist despite all my efforts to banish it. Sometimes it would even remain fixed in space though I pushed my hand through it. If my explanation is correct, it should be able to project on a screen the image of any object one conceives and make it visible. Such an advance would revolutionize all human relations. I am convinced that this wonder can and will be accomplished in time to come; I may add that I have devoted much

空想象的。当有人对我说了一个词，它所指代的物体的形象就会生动地呈现在我面前，有时我都很难区分我看到的东西是不是真实的，这使我感到非常不适和焦虑。我咨询过心理学和生理学专业的学生，没有一个人能给出令人满意的解释。这个病很罕见，似乎是先天性的，因为就我所知，我的哥哥也有类似的困扰。我的结论是，这些幻象是大脑在高度兴奋下对视网膜反射作用的结果。它们当然不是病态或痛苦所产生的幻觉，因为其他方面我很正常，也很冷静。为了说明我的苦恼，假设我目睹了一场葬礼或一些类似的令人神经紧张的场面，然后，不可避免地，在夜深人静的时候，这个场景就会出现在我的眼前，无论我怎么努力都不能将它赶走。有时，即使我伸出手穿过幻象，它仍会停留在空中。如果我的解释是正确的，那么，将大脑所想象的任何物体的图像投射到屏幕上，使其可视化，应该是可能的。这种技术将彻底改变所有的人类关系。我坚信，在不久的将来，这一奇迹能够并且必将实现。补充说一句，我对如何解决这一问题已经进行了很多思考。

thought to the solution of the problem.

To free myself of these tormenting appearances, I tried to concentrate my mind on something else I had seen, and in this way I would often obtain temporary relief; but in order to get it I had to conjure continuously new images. It was not long before I found that I had exhausted all of those at my command; my "reel" had run out, as it were, because I had seen little of the world—only objects in my home and the immediate surroundings. As I performed these mental operations for the second or third time, in order to chase the appearances from my vision, the remedy gradually lost all its force. Then I instinctively commenced to make excursions beyond the limits of the small world of which I had knowledge, and I saw new scenes. These were at first very blurred and indistinct, and would flit away when I tried to concentrate my attention upon them, but by and by I succeeded in fixing them; they gained in strength and distinctness and finally assumed the concreteness of real things. I soon discovered that my best comfort was attained if I simply went on in my vision farther and farther, getting new impressions all the time, and so I began to travel—of course, in my mind. Every night (and sometimes during the day), when alone, I would start on my journeys— see new places, cities and countries—live there, meet people and make friendships and acquaintances and, however unbelievable, it is a fact that they were just as dear to me as those in actual life and not a bit less

第一章 我的早年
I . My Early Life

　　为了摆脱这些折磨人的幻象,我试图去想以前见过的其他事物,通过这种方式,一般我会得到短暂的缓解,但我必须不断想到新的事物。没过多久,我发现我已经用尽了我能想到的所有事物,可以说,我的"胶卷"已经用完了,因为我几乎没有见过什么东西——只有家里和房子周围的一些。每件事物,在脑子里用过两三次后,在将幻象赶出我的视野方面,就逐渐丧失了功效。然后,出于本能,我的思想开始远足,跳出我所了解的小世界的界限,我看到了新的景象。这些景象起初非常模糊,当我试图将注意力集中在它们身上时,它们就会飞走,但渐渐地,我成功地将它们固定了下来,它们的强度和清晰度不断提高,最后呈现出真实事物的样子。我很快发现,如果我的思想一直远行,不断获得新的印象,我就能获得最佳的舒适感。于是我开始旅行——当然,是在我的脑海中。每天晚上(有时是白天),当我独自一人时,我就会开始我的旅行——看看新的地方、城市和国家——在那里生活,遇到各种人,结交朋友,与人熟识,尽管不可思议,但事实上,他们对我来说就跟现实生活中的人一样亲切,充满烟火气。

intense in their manifestations.

This I did constantly until I was about seventeen when my thoughts turned seriously to invention. Then I observed to my delight that I could visualize with the greatest facility. I needed no models, drawings or experiments. I could picture them all as real in my mind. Thus I have been led unconsciously to evolve what I consider a new method of materializing inventive concepts and ideas, which is radically opposite to the purely experimental and is in my opinion ever so much more expeditious and efficient. The moment one constructs a device to carry into practise a crude idea he finds himself unavoidably engrost with the details and defects of the apparatus. As he goes on improving and reconstructing, his force of concentration diminishes and he loses sight of the great underlying principle. Results may be obtained but always at the sacrifice of quality.

My method is different. I do not rush into actual work. When I get an idea I start at once building it up in my imagination. I change the construction, make improvements and operate the device in my mind. It is absolutely immaterial to me whether I run my turbine in thought or test it in my shop. I even note if it is out of balance. There is no difference whatever, the results are the same. In this way I am able to rapidly develop and perfect a conception without touching

这样的情况一直持续到我 17 岁，我开始正儿八经地思考发明。然后我高兴地发现，我可以自如地将想法具象化，不需要模型、图纸或实验。我可以在脑海中想象它们都是真实的。因此，不知不觉中，我发现了一种实现发明概念的新方法，这种方法与纯粹的实验性方法完全相反，在我看来，我的方法更加迅速有效。当一个人打造一个设备来实现一个粗糙的想法时，他会发现自己不可避免地被一些细节和瑕疵所困扰。他得不断改进和重建，注意力就会被分散，甚至对最基本的原理都视而不见了。也许最终也会有成效，但质量方面总是差强人意。

我的方法不同。我不急于付诸实践。当我有了一个想法，马上就会在脑海中构建它，包括设备的改造、优化和运行。对我来说，是在脑海里还是在车间里运行我的涡轮机，并无二样，我甚至会在脑海中记录涡轮机是否失去了平衡。没有任何区别，结果都是一样的。通过这种方式，我能够在不触碰任何东西的情况下迅速发展和完善一个概念。当我把我能想到的所有可能的改进都体现在发明中，并且没有发现任何

anything. When I have gone so far as to embody in the invention every possible improvement I can think of and see no fault anywhere, I put into concrete form this final product of my brain. Invariably my device works as I conceived that it should, and the experiment comes out exactly as I planned it. In twenty years there has not been a single exception. Why should it be otherwise? Engineering, electrical and mechanical, is positive in results. There is scarcely a subject that cannot be mathematically treated and the effects calculated or the results determined beforehand from the available theoretical and practical data. The carrying out into practise of a crude idea as is being generally done is, I hold, nothing but a waste of energy, money and time.

My early affliction had, however, another compensation. The incessant mental exertion developed my powers of observation and enabled me to discover a truth of great importance. I had noted that the appearance of images was always preceded by actual vision of scenes under peculiar and generally very exceptional conditions and I was impelled on each occasion to locate the original impulse. After a while this effort grew to be almost automatic and I gained great facility in connecting cause and effect. Soon I became aware, to my surprise, that every thought I conceived was suggested by an external impression. Not only this but all my actions were prompted in a similar way. In the course of time it became perfectly evident to me that I was merely an

瑕疵时，我才会把我脑海中的成品具象化。这样生产出的设备总是按照我的设想来工作，实验结果也完全按照我的计划进行。20年来，没有一次例外。为什么会有例外呢？工程、电气和机械数据都良好。世间几无一物不可预先进行数学演算，不可基于现有的理论和实践数据计算效果或得出结论。在我看来，将一个不成熟的想法付诸实践的现行做法，只不过是在浪费精力、金钱和时间。

不过，早年的怪病还给了我另一种回报。永不停歇的脑力运动锻炼了我的观察力，让我发现了一个非常重要的真理。我注意到，幻象的出现总是发生在特定或异常情形下我目睹了真实场景之后，而每次我都会驱使自己去追究成因。一段时间后，这几乎变成了自发的行为，我获得了一种能力，能将事情的因果关系轻松地联系起来。令我惊讶的是，很快我就意识到，我的每一个想法都源自某个外界印象，而且，我的所有行动亦如此。随着时间的推移，我越来越明白，我不过是一个被赋予了行动能力的机器人，对感官刺激做出反应，并进行思考和行动。实际上这就是遥控力学的艺术，但迄今为止，还并不完美。然而，其潜在的可能性最终将被证明。

automaton endowed with power of movement, responding to the stimuli of the sense organs and thinking and acting accordingly. The practical result of this was the art of telautomatics which has been so far carried out only in an imperfect manner. Its latent possibilities will, however, be eventually shown. I have been since years planning self-controlled automata and believe that mechanisms can be produced which will act as if possessed of reason, to a limited degree, and will create a revolution in many commercial and industrial departments.

I was about twelve years old when I first succeeded in banishing an image from my vision by wilful effort, but I never had any control over the flashes of light to which I have referred. They were, perhaps, my strangest experience and inexplicable. They usually occurred when I found myself in a dangerous or distressing situation, or when I was greatly exhilarated. In some instances I have seen all the air around me filled with tongues of living flame. Their intensity, instead of diminishing, increased with time and seemingly attained a maximum when I was about twenty-five years old. While in Paris, in 1883, a prominent French manufacturer sent me an invitation to a shooting expedition which I accepted. I had been long confined to the factory and the fresh air had a wonderfully invigorating effect on me. On my return to the city that night I felt a positive sensation that my brain had caught fire. I saw a light as though a small sun was located in it and I past the

多年来,我一直在设计自控机器人,相信可以生产出具有一定推理能力的机器,并将在商业和工业领域掀起一场革命。

差不多12岁时,我第一次通过主观意志,成功地将幻象从我的视野中驱离,但对我曾提到过的闪光情况,仍无能为力。这也许是我最奇怪的经历,令人费解。当我身处危险,或心情沮丧,或极度亢奋时,闪光现象就出现了。有时候,我看到周围的空气充满了熊熊燃烧的火舌。随着时间的推移,这种症状的强度不但没有减弱,反而不断递增,在我大约25岁时达到了峰值。1883年,在巴黎,我接受了一位著名的法国制造商的邀请,出城打靶。我在工厂里待了太长时间,郊外新鲜的空气对我产生了奇妙的兴奋作用。当天晚上回城后,我感觉大脑像着了火。我看到一束光,光亮之中,好像有一个小小的太阳,整晚我都不得不对我饱受折磨的脑袋进行冷敷。终于,闪光的频率和强度开始减弱,但过了三个多星期才完全消退。所以当我第二次受邀时,坚决地回了个"不"!

whole night applying cold compressions to my tortured head. Finally the flashes diminished in frequency and force but it took more than three weeks before they wholly subsided. When a second invitation was extended to me my answer was an emphatic NO!

These luminous phenomena still manifest themselves from time to time, as when a new idea opening up possibilities strikes me, but they are no longer exciting, being of relatively small intensity. When I close my eyes I invariably observe first, a background of very dark and uniform blue, not unlike the sky on a clear but starless night. In a few seconds this field becomes animated with innumerable scintillating flakes of green, arranged in several layers and advancing towards me. Then there appears, to the right, a beautiful pattern of two systems of parallel and closely spaced lines, at right angles to one another, in all sorts of colors with yellow-green and gold predominating. Immediately thereafter the lines grow brighter and the whole is thickly sprinkled with dots of twinkling light. This picture moves slowly across the field of vision and in about ten seconds vanishes to the left, leaving behind a ground of rather unpleasant and inert grey which quickly gives way to a billowy sea of clouds, seemingly trying to mould themselves in living shapes. It is curious that I cannot project a form into this grey until the second phase is reached. Every time, before falling asleep, images of persons or objects flit before my view. When I see them I know that I

这种闪光现象仍时不时地出现，比如我突然有了一个新的想法，觉得有各种可能性时，但已经不再那么刺激，强度也相对较小了。当我闭上眼睛，总是先浮现一片匀色的深蓝背景，跟晴朗无星的夜空如出一辙。几秒钟后，这片区域变得生动起来，无数闪烁的绿色碎片，分几层排列，向我推进。然后，右边出现了一个美丽图案，由两组线条组成，彼此呈直角，每组线条内，又有多条紧密排列的平行线条，五颜六色，且以黄绿色和金色最显眼。紧接着，这些线条变得越发明亮，整个图案密密麻麻地布满了闪烁的光点。图案在我眼前慢慢移动，大约十秒钟后消失在左边，留下一片令人相当不快的、沉闷乏味的灰色，很快又被一片波涛汹涌的云海所取代，似乎挣扎着要变化成各种活物的形状。奇怪的是，要是没有睡意，我是没办法在这片灰色中生出任何形状的。每次入睡前，各种人或物的形象都会在我眼前闪现。这时，我知道我就快要睡着了。但如果没有，就意味着将彻夜不眠。

am about to lose consciousness. If they are absent and refuse to come it means a sleepless night.

To what an extent imagination played a part in my early life I may illustrate by another odd experience. Like most children I was fond of jumping and developed an intense desire to support myself in the air. Occasionally a strong wind richly charged with oxygen blew from the mountains rendering my body as light as cork and then I would leap and float in space for a long time. It was a delightful sensation and my disappointment was keen when later I undeceived myself.

During that period I contracted many strange likes, dislikes and habits, some of which I can trace to external impressions while others are unaccountable. I had a violent aversion against the earrings of women but other ornaments, as bracelets, pleased me more or less according to design. The sight of a pearl would almost give me a fit but I was fascinated with the glitter of crystals or objects with sharp edges and plane surfaces. I would not touch the hair of other people except, perhaps, at the point of a revolver. I would get a fever by looking at a peach and if a piece of camphor was anywhere in the house it caused me the keenest discomfort. Even now I am not insensible to some of these upsetting impulses. When I drop little squares of paper in a dish filled with liquid, I always sense a peculiar and awful taste in my mouth.

第一章 我的早年
I . My Early Life

想象力在我早年生活中发挥了多大的作用,我可以通过另一个奇特的经历来说明。像大多数孩子一样,我喜欢跳跃,并产生了一种强烈的愿望——想要能在空中停留。偶尔会有一阵富含氧气的强风从山上吹来,使我的身体像软木塞一样轻盈,然后我就可以跳起来,在空中飘浮很长时间。这是一种令人愉快的感觉,而当我从幻想中缓过神来时,感到非常失落。

那段时间里,我染上了许多奇怪的喜好和习惯,其中一些可以追溯到某种外在原因,而另一些则无法解释。我对女人的耳环十分反感,但对其他装饰品,如手镯,视设计不同,或多或少都会喜欢。看到珍珠会让我发狂,但我却会被闪闪发光的水晶或棱角分明、表明平滑的物体所吸引。我不会去碰别人的头发,除非被人用枪抵着。一看到桃子我就会发烧。如果房子里有一块樟脑丸,会使我感到强烈的不适。即使是现在,我也无法对我的一些怪癖无动于衷。当我把小方块碎纸丢到盛满汤汁的盘子里时,总能感觉到嘴里有一种恶心的怪味。我数着走路的步数,计算着汤碟、咖啡杯和食物的体积,否则我的这顿饭就索然无味。我的所有日常行为重复的次数都必须能被三整除,如果不是,我会强迫自己重

I counted the steps in my walks and calculated the cubical contents of soup plates, coffee cups and pieces of food—otherwise my meal was unenjoyable. All repeated acts or operations I performed had to be divisible by three and if I mist I felt impelled to do it all over again, even if it took hours.

Up to the age of eight years, my character was weak and vacillating. I had neither courage or strength to form a firm resolve. My feelings came in waves and surges and vibrated unceasingly between extremes. My wishes were of consuming force and like the heads of the hydra, they multiplied. I was oppressed by thoughts of pain in life and death and religious fear. I was swayed by superstitious belief and lived in constant dread of the spirit of evil, of ghosts and ogres and other unholy monsters of the dark. Then, all at once, there came a tremendous change which altered the course of my whole existence.

Of all things I liked books the best. My father had a large library and whenever I could manage I tried to satisfy my passion for reading. He did not permit it and would fly into a rage when he caught me in the act. He hid the candles when he found that I was reading in secret. He did not want me to spoil my eyes. But I obtained tallow, made the wicking and cast the sticks into tin forms, and every night I would bush the keyhole and the cracks and read, often till dawn, when all others

新做一遍，哪怕要花上几个小时。

直到8岁，我的性格都很优柔寡断。我既没有勇气，也没有能力去做决断。我的情绪跌宕起伏，在两个极端之间不停摇摆。我的欲望十分旺盛，像九头蛇的头一样，恣意生长。生与死的痛苦和对宗教的恐惧折磨着我，迷信的观念左右着我，一直活在对邪灵、鬼魂、食人魔以及其他暗黑恶怪的恐怖阴影中。然后，突然之间，一次巨变修正了我整个的人生轨迹。

在所有的事物中，我最喜欢的是书。我父亲有一个很大的藏书室，只要一有机会我就会去读书。可他不允许我这样做，一旦被他逮个正着，他就会大发雷霆。当他发现我在偷偷看书，就把蜡烛藏了起来。他不想我什么书都看。但我弄到了牛油，制作了灯芯，自制了蜡烛棒，每天晚上我都会堵住钥匙孔和门缝，在里面看书，常常看到天亮，那时其他人都还在睡梦中，而母亲已经开始了她一天繁重的工作。有一

slept and my mother started on her arduous daily task. On one occasion I came across a novel entitled "Abafi", a Serbian translation of a well known Hungarian writer, Josika. This work somehow awakened my dormant powers of will and I began to practise self-control. At first my resolutions faded like snow in April, but in a little while I conquered my weakness and felt a pleasure I never knew before—that of doing as I willed. In the course of time this vigorous mental exercise became second nature. At the outset my wishes had to be subdued but gradually desire and will grew to be identical. After years of such discipline I gained so complete a mastery over myself that I toyed with passions which have meant destruction to some of the strongest men. At a certain age I contracted a mania for gambling which greatly worried my parents. To sit down to a game of cards was for me the quintessence of pleasure. My father led an exemplary life and could not excuse the senseless waste of time and money in which I indulged. I had a strong resolve but my philosophy was bad. I would say to him, "I can stop whenever I please but is it worth while to give up that which I would purchase with the joys of Paradise?" On frequent occasions he gave vent to his anger and contempt but my mother was different. She understood the character of men and knew that one's salvation could only be brought about thru his own efforts. One afternoon, I remember, when I had lost all my money and was craving for a game, she came to me with a roll

第一章 我的早年
I . My Early Life

次,我偶然读到一本名为《阿巴菲》①的小说,是匈牙利著名作家约西卡(Josika)的塞尔维亚语译本。这部作品不知何故唤醒了我沉睡的意志力,我开始练习自我控制。起初,我的决心像四月的雪一样转瞬消融,但没过多久,我战胜了自己的弱点,感受到了一种前所未有的快乐——做自己想做的事。随着时间的推移,这种高强度的精神锻炼成了我的第二天性。一开始,我必须要压制欲望,但渐渐地,欲望和意志变得一致。经过多年训练,我已经做到能完全自控,哪怕是面对一些可以毁人一生的欲望,也可以进退自如。有段时间,我染上了赌博,这让我的父母非常担心。坐下来打牌对我来说是最大的快乐。我父亲的生活堪称楷模,他无法原谅我沉溺于打牌,毫无意义地浪费时间和金钱。虽然我有很强的自制力,但我的人生观却很糟糕。我对他说:"我可以随时停止,但这种天堂都买不到的快乐,我就这么放弃,值得吗?"为此他多次大发雷霆,对我嗤之以鼻,但母亲却不同。她洞悉人性,知道一个人的救赎只能通过自己来实现。我记得那是一个下午,我输光了所有的钱,正渴望着再赌一场时,她拿着一沓钞票走到我面前说:"去玩吧。把我们的钱输光,越快越好。我知道你会征服它的。"她是对的。我当场改过自新,只是遗憾这种欲望没再强烈一百倍。我不仅战

---

① 写于十九世纪的匈牙利历史小说,讲述了匈牙利骑士阿巴菲弃恶从善的故事。

of bills and said, "Go and enjoy yourself. The sooner you lose all we possess the better it will be. I know that you will get over it." She was right. I conquered my passion then and there and only regretted that it had not been a hundred times as strong. I not only vanquished but tore it from my heart so as not to leave even a trace of desire. Ever since that time I have been as indifferent to any form of gambling as to picking teeth.

During another period I smoked excessively, threatening to ruin my health. Then my will asserted itself and I not only stopt but destroyed all inclination. Long ago I suffered from heart trouble until I discovered that it was due to the innocent cup of coffee I consumed every morning. I discontinued at once, although I confess it was not an easy task. In this way I checked and bridled other habits and passions and have not only preserved my life but derived an immense amount of satisfaction from what most men would consider privation and sacrifice.

After finishing the studies at the Polytechnic Institute and University I had a complete nervous breakdown and while the malady lasted I observed many phenomena strange and unbelievable.

第一章 我的早年
I . My Early Life

胜了它，而且把它从我的心中连根拔掉，再无半点眷恋。从那时起，我对任何形式的赌博都像对剔牙一样完全没了兴趣。

还有一段时间，我烟抽得很凶，危害到了我的健康。后来我的意志力证明了自己，我不仅戒了烟，而且根除了所有的不良嗜好。很久以前，我曾患过心脏病，我发现这跟我每天早上喝的那杯无辜的咖啡有关，尽管我承认这不是一件容易的事，但我还是戒掉了。通过这种方式，我约束和克服了其他的坏习惯，这不仅保住了我的生命，而且从大多数人认为是徒劳无益的事情中获得了巨大的满足。

在完成格拉茨理工大学的学业后，我的精神彻底崩溃，在患病期间，我观察到了许多匪夷所思的现象。

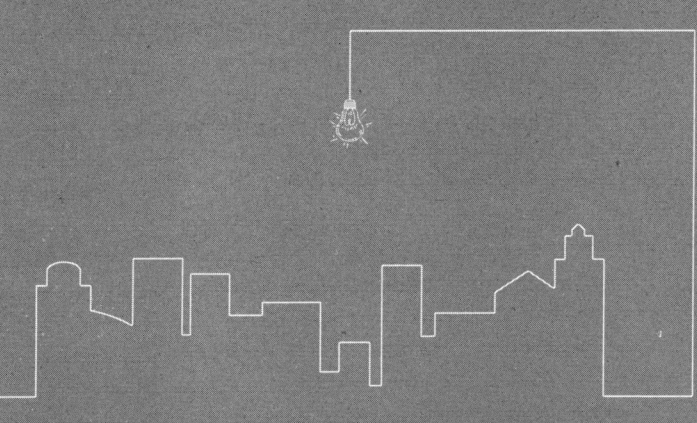

II . My First Efforts in Invention

第二章 发明初体验

I shall dwell briefly on these extraordinary experiences, on account of their possible interest to students of psychology and physiology and also because this period of agony was of the greatest consequence on my mental development and subsequent labors. But it is indispensable to first relate the circumstances and conditions which preceded them and in which might be found their partial explanation.

From childhood I was compelled to concentrate attention upon myself. This caused me much suffering but, to my present view, it was a blessing in disguise for it has taught me to appreciate the inestimable value of introspection in the preservation of life, as well as a means of achievement. The pressure of occupation and the incessant stream of impressions pouring into our consciousness through all the gateways of knowledge make modern existence hazardous in many ways. Most persons are so absorbed in the contemplation of the outside world that they are wholly oblivious to what is passing on within themselves.

The premature death of millions is primarily traceable to this cause. Even among those who exercise care it is a common mistake to avoid imaginary, and ignore the real dangers. And what is true of an individual also applies, more or less, to a people as a whole. Witness, in illustration, the prohibition movement. A drastic, if not unconstitutional, measure is now being put through in this country to

第二章 发明初体验
Ⅱ. My First Efforts in Invention

对于这些不寻常的经历，我还想唠叨几句，一方面，心理学和生理学专业的学生可能会感兴趣，另一方面，这段痛苦的经历与我的心智发展及后期研究有莫大的关系。但首先，我必须叙述一下这些经历之前的情况，或可找到一些因果关联。

从孩提时代起，我就被迫专注于内心，这让我饱受煎熬，但现在看来，却是因祸得福，因为我懂得了，不管是对人生，还是作为一种成功之道，内省都有着不可估量的价值。工作的压力，以及通过知识门户源源不断涌入我们意识的各种外界印象，使现代人的生存在许多方面变得岌岌可危。大多数人都沉浸在对外部世界的思考中，以至于完全无视自己内心发生了些什么。

数百万人的早逝都可以追溯到这一主要原因。即使在那些注重养生的人中，避免去想象而忽视了真正的危险，也是一个常见的误区。对个人而言如此，对整个国家而言亦是如此。拿禁酒运动为例，我们国家目前正在实施一项不违宪但却很极端的措施以限制酒精的消费。然而，事实却是，咖啡、茶、烟草、口香糖和其他刺激物，即使未成年也可以自由享用，从死亡人

prevent the consumption of alcohol and yet it is a positive fact that coffee, tea, tobacco, chewing gum and other stimulants, which are freely indulged in even at the tender age, are vastly more injurious to the national body, judging from the number of those who succumb. So, for instance, during my student years I gathered from the published necrologues in Vienna, the home of coffee drinkers, that deaths from heart trouble sometimes reached sixty-seven percent of the total. Similar observations might probably be made in cities where the consumption of tea is excessive. These delicious beverages super excite and gradually exhaust the fine fibers of the brain. They also interfere seriously with arterial circulation and should be enjoyed all the more sparingly as their deleterious effects are slow and imperceptible. Tobacco, on the other hand, is conducive to easy and pleasant thinking and detracts from the intensity and concentration necessary to all original and vigorous effort of the intellect. Chewing gum is helpful for a short while but soon drains the glandular system and inflicts irreparable damage, not to speak of the revulsion it creates. Alcohol in small quantities is an excellent tonic, but is toxic in its action when absorbed in larger amounts, quite immaterial as to whether it is taken in as whiskey or produced in the stomach from sugar. But it should not be overlooked that all these are great eliminators assisting Nature, as they do, in upholding her stern but just law of the survival of the fittest.

数来看，这些对国民身体的危害要大得多。例如，在我的学生时代，我从维也纳——这个咖啡爱好者的故乡公布的死亡统计中得知，心脏病的死亡人数有时竟达到死亡总数的67%。在过度饮用茶叶的城市，可能也会有类似的发现。这些美味的饮料会使大脑过度兴奋，逐渐损伤大脑的神经纤维。另外，还会严重干扰血液循环，鉴于这些副作用进程缓慢、难以察觉，所以更应该少喝。而烟草呢，有助于轻松愉悦的思考，但对于所有原创性的复杂思维所必需的高强度和专注力，却是有损伤的。嚼口香糖在短时间内有用，但很快就会耗尽腺体分泌，造成无法弥补的损害，更不用说引起的恶心感了。至于喝酒，小酌怡情，但一旦过量，则十分有害，至于是作为威士忌摄入还是由糖在胃里产生，并无区别。但不应忽视的是，所有这些都是极好的过滤器，帮助大自然维护其严酷而公正的适者生存法则。热衷于改革的人们也应该注意到，人类永远都是刚愎自用的，相比强制约束，放任自流似乎更可取。

Eager reformers should also be mindful of the eternal perversity of mankind which makes the indifferent "laissez-faire" by far preferable to enforced restraint.

The truth about this is that we need stimulants to do our best work under present living conditions, and that we must exercise moderation and control our appetites and inclinations in every direction. That is what I have been doing for many years, in this way maintaining myself young in body and mind. Abstinence was not always to my liking but I find ample reward in the agreeable experiences I am now making. Just in the hope of converting some to my precepts and convictions I will recall one or two.

A short time ago I was returning to my hotel. It was a bitter cold night, the ground slippery, and no taxi to be had. Half a block behind me followed another man, evidently as anxious as myself to get under cover. Suddenly my legs went up in the air. In the same instant there was a flash in my brain, the nerves responded, the muscles contracted, I swung through 180 degrees and landed on my hands. I resumed my walk as though nothing had happened when the stranger caught up with me. "How old are you?" he asked, surveying me critically. "Oh, about fifty-nine," I replied. "What of it?" "Well," said he, "I have seen a cat do this but never a man." About a month since I wanted to order new

第二章 发明初体验
II. My First Efforts in Invention

事实上,就当下的生活条件而言,我们需要一些刺激物才能将工作完成得更好,但与此同时,我们必须学会适度,合理控制我们的各种欲望。这么多年来,我一直奉行此道,以保持自己的身心健康。禁欲并不总是为我所爱,但从我现行的生活方式中,我得到了充足的回报。下面我将说一说我的一两件逸事,希望你们当中有人会转而接受我的信条。

不久前,一个寒冷的夜晚,我在回酒店的路上,路面很滑,街上一辆出租车都没有。在我身后半个街区的距离,跟着一个人,显然他和我一样急着回家。突然间,我脚下打滑,双腿腾空而起,与此同时,我的大脑中闪过一道光,神经迅速做出反应,肌肉收缩,在空中我旋转了180度,双手撑地。我站起身来,若无其事地继续行走,好像什么都没有发生过。这时候,那个人从后面追上我,一边上下打量着我,一边问道:"您多大了?""噢,59岁了,"我答道,"怎么了?""嗯,"他说,"我见过猫这样做,但从未见过人能这样做。"大概一个月后,我想订一副新眼镜,于是去找了一位眼科医生,他对我进行了视力测

eyeglasses and went to an oculist who put me through the usual tests. He looked at me incredulously as I read off with ease the smallest print at considerable distance. But when I told him that I was past sixty he gasped in astonishment. Friends of mine often remark that my suits fit me like gloves but they do not know that all my clothing is made to measurements which were taken nearly 35 years ago and never changed. During this same period my weight has not varied one pound.

In this connection I may tell a funny story. One evening, in the winter of 1885, Mr. Edison, Edward H. Johnson, the President of the Edison Illuminating Company, Mr. Batchellor, Manager of the works, and myself entered a little place opposite 65 Fifth Avenue where the offices of the company were located. Someone suggested guessing weights and I was induced to step on a scale. Edison felt me all over and said: "Tesla weighs 152 lbs. to an ounce," and he guest it exactly. Stripped I weighed 142 lbs. And that is still my weight. I whispered to Mr. Johnson: "How is it possible that Edison could guess my weight so closely?" "Well," he said, lowering his voice. "I will tell you, confidentially, but you must not say anything. He was employed for a long time in a Chicago slaughter-house where he weighed thousands of hogs every day! That's why." My friend, the Honorable Chauncey M. Depew, tells of an Englishman on whom he sprung one of his original anecdotes and who listened with a puzzled expression but—a year

第二章 发明初体验
II. My First Efforts in Invention

试。看到我在很远的地方轻松地辨出最小的标记,他脸上露出难以置信的表情。当我告诉他我已经快 60 岁时,他更是惊得目瞪口呆。朋友们经常说我的衣服十分合身,但他们不知道的是,我所有的衣服都是按照 35 年前的尺寸定做的,从未改变过。同样的,我的体重也没有变过哪怕一磅。

  关于这一点,我可以讲一件趣事。1885 年冬天的一个晚上,爱迪生先生、爱迪生照明公司的总裁爱德华·约翰逊先生、工厂经理巴切勒先生和我走进第五大道 65 号对面的一个小地方,那里是公司办公室的所在地。有人建议来猜体重,怂恿我站上体重秤。爱迪生上下打量了我一番,然后说:"特斯拉重 152 磅,上下差不了 1 盎司。"他猜得很准,我除去衣服,净重 142 磅,至今仍是。我低声问约翰逊先生:"爱迪生怎么能把我的体重猜得这么准呢?""嗯,"他压低声音说,"我悄悄告诉你,但你不能往外说,他曾在芝加哥的一家屠宰场工作过很长时间,在那里,他每天都要称几千头猪的重量!这下你懂了吧。"我朋友昌西·迪普告诉过我,他曾跟一个英国人讲过一件关于他自己的趣事,当时那个英国人听得不明所以,但一年后明白了笑点所在,笑得不能自已。坦白说,我花了更多的时间才领会到约翰逊这番话的笑点。

later—laughed out loud. I will frankly confess it took me longer than that to appreciate Johnson's joke.

Now, my well being is simply the result of a careful and measured mode of living and perhaps the most astonishing thing is that three times in my youth I was rendered by illness a hopeless physical wreck and given up by physicians. More than this, through ignorance and lightheartedness, I got into all sorts of difficulties, dangers and scrapes from which I extricated myself as by enchantment. I was almost drowned a dozen times; was nearly boiled alive and just mist being cremated. I was entombed, lost and frozen. I had hair-breadth escapes from mad dogs, hogs, and other wild animals. I past through dreadful diseases and met with all kinds of odd mishaps and that I am hale and hearty today seems like a miracle. But as I recall these incidents to my mind I feel convinced that my preservation was not altogether accidental.

An inventor's endeavor is essentially lifesaving. Whether he harnesses forces, improves devices, or provides new comforts and conveniences, he is adding to the safety of our existence. He is also better qualified than the average individual to protect himself in peril, for he is observant and resourceful. If I had no other evidence that I was, in a measure, possessed of such qualities I would find it in these

第二章 发明初体验
II. My First Efforts in Invention

所以，我现在的健康就是源自我谨慎而有节制的生活方式，说出来你们可能不信，我在年轻的时候，曾三次被疾病折磨得体无完肤，连医生都无能为力。不仅如此，由于无知和轻率，我陷入过各种困难、危险和挫折之中，但我每每又逃出生天。我有十几次差点被淹死，有次差点被开水活活烫死，还差一点被火烧死；我被掩埋过，走丢过，冻僵过；我曾从疯狗、野猪和其他野生动物口中侥幸逃脱过；我经历过可怕的疾病，遇到过各种各样的怪事，今天我还能安然无恙地活着，简直就是个奇迹。但当我回忆起这些事情时，我确信，我能活下来并不完全是偶然。

发明家的努力本质上是为了拯救生命。无论是利用外力，还是改进设备，抑或是提供新的舒适和便利，都是在保障我们的生命安全。而且，发明家们善于观察，足智多谋，因此也比一般人更有能力在危险中保护自己。我没有其他证据证明我在某种程度上拥有这样的品质，但从我的个人经历中能找到些蛛丝马迹。这里我举一两个例子，读者可以自行判断。我在 14 岁

personal experiences. The reader will be able to judge for himself if I mention one or two instances. On one occasion, when about 14 years old, I wanted to scare some friends who were bathing with me. My plan was to dive under a long floating structure and slip out quietly at the other end. Swimming and diving came to me as naturally as to a duck and I was confident that I could perform the feat. Accordingly I plunged into the water and, when out of view, turned around and proceeded rapidly towards the opposite side. Thinking that I was safely beyond the structure, I rose to the surface but to my dismay struck a beam. Of course, I quickly dived and forged ahead with rapid strokes until my breath was beginning to give out. Rising for the second time, my head came again in contact with a beam. Now I was becoming desperate. However, summoning all my energy, I made a third frantic attempt but the result was the same. The torture of suppressed breathing was getting unendurable, my brain was reeling and I felt myself sinking. At that moment, when my situation seemed absolutely hopeless, I experienced one of those flashes of light and the structure above me appeared before my vision. I either discerned or guessed that there was a little space between the surface of the water and the boards resting on the beams and, with consciousness nearly gone, I floated up, pressed my mouth close to the planks and managed to inhale a little air, unfortunately mingled with a spray of water which nearly choked me. Several times I

的时候，有一次，想吓唬下和我一起游泳的朋友。河面上浮着一个长长的建筑物，我的计划是先潜到下面，然后从另一端悄悄地游出来。游泳和潜水对我来说简直是小菜一碟，我有信心完成这一壮举。于是，我扎进水里，趁没人注意，转身迅速向建筑物另一头游去。我以为自己已经安全地游过了建筑物，于是浮出水面，但令我惊恐的是，我撞到了一块横梁。当然了，我迅速下潜，快速划水前进，直到快憋不住气了，才第二次上浮，但头又碰到了横梁。我开始绝望了，无论如何，我汇聚所有的力气，近乎抓狂地第三次上浮，但结果是一样的。憋气憋得越来越难受，大脑也昏昏沉沉的，我感到自己在下沉。此时的处境似乎已再无生机，但千钧一发之际，那种闪光现象又出现了，建筑物的幻象浮现在我眼前。不管是看到的，还是猜到的，在水面和横梁上方的木板之间有一点空隙，我在失去意识前，浮了上去，把嘴贴近木板，设法吸进了一点空气，但与此同时，一口水灌进我嘴里，差点没呛死。感觉像在梦里，我重复着这个过程，直到剧烈跳动的心脏平缓下来，才恢复了镇定。在那之后，我又尝试了几次潜水，但都以失败告终，完全失去了方向感，不过，最终我还是成功地逃离了困境，当时我的朋友都觉得我活不成了，正准备打捞我的尸体。

repeated this procedure as in a dream until my heart, which was racing at a terrible rate, quieted down and I gained composure. After that I made a number of unsuccessful dives, having completely lost the sense of direction, but finally succeeded in getting out of the trap when my friends had already given me up and were fishing for my body.

That bathing season was spoiled for me through recklessness but I soon forgot the lesson and only two years later I fell into a worse predicament. There was a large flour mill with a dam across the river near the city where I was studying at that time. As a rule the height of the water was only two or three inches above the dam and to swim out to it was a sport not very dangerous in which I often indulged. One day I went alone to the river to enjoy myself as usual. When I was a short distance from the masonry, however, I was horrified to observe that the water had risen and was carrying me along swiftly. I tried to get away but it was too late. Luckily, though, I saved myself from being swept over by taking hold of the wall with both hands. The pressure against my chest was great and I was barely able to keep my head above the surface. Not a soul was in sight and my voice was lost in the roar of the fall. Slowly and gradually I became exhausted and unable to withstand the strain longer. Just as I was about to let go, to be dashed against the rocks below, I saw in a flash of light a familiar diagram illustrating the hydraulic principle that the pressure of a fluid in motion

第二章 发明初体验
II . My First Efforts in Invention

　　我的鲁莽让那年的游泳季成了一场噩梦,但很快我就忘记了这个教训,仅仅两年后,我陷入了更糟糕的困境。在我当时学习的城市附近,有一条河,河边有个大型磨坊,河上建了个水坝。一般来说,河水只比坝体高出两三英寸,往坝体处游并不是一项十分危险的运动,我对此乐此不疲。有一天,我像往常一样独自去河里游泳。然而,当我离坝体不远时,我惊恐地发现水位上涨了,正迅速地把我卷向坝底。我试图逃跑,但为时已晚。幸运的是,我双手紧紧扣住了坝壁,这才使自己没有被水冲走。我的胸腔承受着巨大的压力,勉强才能将头露出水面。一个人影也看不见,我的声音也湮灭在咆哮的水流声中。渐渐地,我变得筋疲力尽,无法再承受这种压力。正当我准备放手,任凭被冲到坝底的岩石上时,在闪光之中,我看到了一张熟悉的液压原理图表,即运动中流体的压力与受力面积成正比,于是我下意识地将身体转向左侧。水压奇迹般地变小了,我发现用这个姿势抵御水流的冲击要轻松些。但危险仍未消除,我知道我迟早会被冲下去,哪怕有人发现我,也无法及时赶到我身边救我。现在我双手都很灵活,但那时候,我是左撇子,

is proportionate to the area exposed, and automatically I turned on my left side. As if by magic the pressure was reduced and I found it comparatively easy in that position to resist the force of the stream. But the danger still confronted me. I knew that sooner or later I would be carried down, as it was not possible for any help to reach me in time, even if I attracted attention. I am ambidextrous now but then I was lefthanded and had comparatively little strength in my right arm. For this reason I did not dare to turn on the other side to rest and nothing remained but to slowly push my body along the dam. I had to get away from the mill towards which my face was turned as the current there was much swifter and deeper. It was a long and painful ordeal and I came near to failing at its very end for I was confronted with a depression in the masonry. I managed to get over with the last ounce of my force and fell in a swoon when I reached the bank, where I was found. I had torn virtually all the skin from my left side and it took several weeks before the fever subsided and I was well. These are only two of many instances but they may be sufficient to show that had it not been for the inventor's instinct I would not have lived to tell this tale.

Interested people have often asked me how and when I began to invent. This I can only answer from my present recollection in the light of which the first attempt I recall was rather ambitious for it involved the invention of an apparatus and a method. In the former I was anticipated

第二章 发明初体验
II. My First Efforts in Invention

右臂几乎没什么力量。因此,我不敢将身体转向右侧,别无他法,只能紧贴坝壁,一点一点往岸边挪。我的脸是朝着磨坊的,那边的水更深,水流更急,我必须远离那儿。这是一场漫长而痛苦的磨难,快到岸边时,坝体有一处低洼,我差点就功亏一篑了。用尽最后一丝力气,我才上了岸,然后立马昏了过去。后来有人发现了我。当时,我的左侧身体被水流冲得几乎体无完肤,花了好几个星期才退了烧,身体才慢慢恢复过来。像这样的事例很多,这里只枚举一二,但足以说明,如果不是因为发明家的天性,我可能活不到今天来讲这个故事。

对我感兴趣的人经常问我,我是如何以及何时走上发明之路的。这个嘛,我只能根据现有的回忆来回答,我记得,我的第一次尝试相当雄心勃勃,涉及一种装置的发明和一种方法的诞生。前者是意料之中,而后者纯属巧合。事情是这样的,我

but the latter was original. It happened in this way. One of my playmates had come into the possession of a hook and fishing-tackle which created quite an excitement in the village, and the next morning all started out to catch frogs. I was left alone and deserted owing to a quarrel with this boy. I had never seen a real hook and pictured it as something wonderful, endowed with peculiar qualities, and was despairing not to be one of the party. Urged by necessity, I somehow got hold of a piece of soft iron wire, hammered the end to a sharp point between two stones, bent it into shape, and fastened it to a strong string. I then cut a rod, gathered some bait, and went down to the brook where there were frogs in abundance. But I could not catch any and was almost discouraged when it occurred to me to dangle the empty hook in front of a frog sitting on a stump. At first he collapsed but by and by his eyes bulged out and became bloodshot, he swelled to twice his normal size and made a vicious snap at the hook.

Immediately I pulled him up. I tried the same thing again and again and the method proved infallible. When my comrades, who in spite of their fine outfit had caught nothing, came to me they were green with envy. For a long time I kept my secret and enjoyed the monopoly but finally yielded to the spirit of Christmas. Every boy could then do the same and the following summer brought disaster to the frogs.

的一个玩伴得到了一个鱼钩和钓具，这在村子里引起了一阵骚动，第二天早上，所有的小伙伴都出发去抓青蛙。由于之前和这个男孩争吵过，我被孤立了，独自一人。我从来没有见过真正的鱼钩，我把它想象成一种奇妙的东西，具有独特的品质。不能和他们一起玩，我绝望至极。实在没有办法，我不知从哪搞到了一根软铁丝，用两块石头把铁丝一端锤得尖尖的，然后弯成个钩子形状，系在一根结实的绳子上。然后我砍了根竹竿，收集了一些饵，来到小河边。那里的青蛙可多了，但我一只都没钓上来，都快泄气了。有只青蛙坐在一个树桩上，我索性把空钩子悬在它面前晃，起初，它并没有搭理我，但渐渐地，它的眼睛鼓了起来，充满了血丝，身体胀到正常大小的两倍，恶狠狠地咬住了钩子。

我迅速把它拉了上来，一次又一次，我尝试同样的方法，事实证明这个方法百试不爽。我的小伙伴们尽管装备精良，却一无所获，他们看到我时，简直羡慕得要死。在很长一段时间里，我一直保守着这个秘密，享受着这个专利，直到圣诞节来临，才告诉了他们。然后每个男孩都如法炮制，接下来的夏天，青蛙们遭了大殃。

In my next attempt I seem to have acted under the first instinctive impulse which later dominated me—to harness the energies of nature to the service of man. I did this through the medium of May-bugs—or June-bugs as they are called in America—which were a veritable pest in that country and sometimes broke the branches of trees by the sheer weight of their bodies. The bushes were black with them. I would attach as many as four of them to a crosspiece, rotably arranged on a thin spindle, and transmit the motion of the same to a large disc and so derive considerable "power". These creatures were remarkably efficient, for once they were started they had no sense to stop and continued whirling for hours and hours and the hotter it was the harder they worked. All went well until a strange boy came to the place. He was the son of a retired officer in the Austrian Army. That urchin ate May-bugs alive and enjoyed them as though they were the finest blue-point oysters. That disgusting sight terminated my endeavors in this promising field and I have never since been able to touch a May-bug or any other insect for that matter.

After that, I believe, I undertook to take apart and assemble the clocks of my grandfather. In the former operation I was always successful but often failed in the latter. So it came that he brought my work to a sudden halt in a manner not too delicate and it took thirty years before I tackled another clockwork again. Shortly thereafter I went

第二章 发明初体验
II . My First Efforts in Invention

我的第二次尝试，似乎是遵循本能，即利用自然之力以泽众生的本能，这一点，是我之后的发明一直坚持的。这次的尝试是关于五月甲虫的，在美国也被称为六月虫，这种虫子在美国是名副其实的害虫，有时会因为自身的重量而压断树枝，灌木丛中黑压压的到处都是它们的身影。我捉了四只固定在一个横杆上，把横杆安在一根可以旋转的细轴上，用它们来带动大转盘旋转，从而获得相当大的"能量"。这些虫子非常高效，一旦开始工作，就不会停下来，一直旋转几个小时，天气越热工作得就越卖力。本来一切都很顺利，直到一个奇怪的男孩来了，他父亲是奥地利军队的一名退役军官。那个顽童生吃了五月甲虫，就好像它们是最美味的蓝点牡蛎一样。这一令人恶心的场面就此打断了我在这一领域的发展，从那以后，我再也无法直视五月甲虫或其他任何昆虫了。

再然后，我开始拆卸并组装我祖父的钟表。在拆卸这一块我很在行，但组装却经常以失败告终。于是，祖父毫不客气地阻止了我，在那之后的30年里，我再也没动过钟表。既然不让碰钟表，很快我就开始制作气枪，这种气枪要用到一根空心管、一个活塞和两个麻纤维团做成的塞子。开枪时，活塞抵住腹部，

into the manufacture of a kind of pop-gun which comprised a hollow tube, a piston, and two plugs of hemp. When firing the gun, the piston was pressed against the stomach and the tube was pushed back quickly with both hands. The air between the plugs was comprest and raised to high temperature and one of them was expelled with a loud report. The art consisted in selecting a tube of the proper taper from the hollow stalks. I did very well with that gun but my activities interfered with the window panes in our house and met with painful discouragement. If I remember rightly, I then took to carving swords from pieces of furniture which I could conveniently obtain. At that time I was under the sway of the Serbian national poetry and full of admiration for the feats of the heroes. I used to spend hours in mowing down my enemies in the form of corn-stalks which ruined the crops and netted me several spankings from my mother. Moreover these were not of the formal kind but the genuine article.

I had all this and more behind me before I was six years old and had past through one year of elementary school in the village of Smiljan where I was born. At this juncture we moved to the little city of Gospic nearby. This change of residence was like a calamity to me. It almost broke my heart to part from our pigeons, chickens and sheep, and our magnificent flock of geese which used to rise to the clouds in the morning and return from the feeding grounds at sundown in

第二章 发明初体验
Ⅱ. My First Efforts in Invention

双手迅速把空心管往回拉。塞子之间的空气被压缩，温度升高，其中一个塞子在"砰"的一声中被射出。这把枪的制作关键在于挑选一个粗细合适的空心管。我那把枪就做得很好，但我们家的窗玻璃却因此遭了殃，我也受到了严厉的呵斥。如果没记错的话，后来，我又迷上了刻剑，直接在随手可得的家具上取材。那时，我深受塞尔维亚民族诗歌的影响，对英雄们的壮举充满了敬佩之情。我常常花上几个小时，把玉米秆当成敌人来砍，因为这一毁坏庄稼的举动，我挨了母亲好几顿揍。以上种种，都绝非信口开河，而是有凭有据。

诸如此类的事情，贯穿了我 6 岁之前的生活，然后，我上小学了。我是在斯米良村上的一年级，那也是我出生的地方。后来，我们搬到了附近的戈斯皮奇小城。这次迁居对我来说就像是一场灾难。离开了我的鸽子、鸡和羊，还有宏伟的鹅群，我的心几乎要碎了，它们踏着晨露出门觅食，在日落时分排着战斗队形返回，队形是如此完美，足以让当今最好的飞行中队相形见绌。而在我们的新家里，我就像一个囚犯，只能透过百

battle formation, so perfect that it would have put a squadron of the best aviators of the present day to shame. In our new house I was but a prisoner, watching the strange people I saw through the window blinds. My bashfulness was such that I would rather have faced a roaring lion than one of the city dudes who strolled about. But my hardest trial came on Sunday when I had to dress up and attend the service. There I meet with an accident, the mere thought of which made my blood curdle like sour milk for years afterwards. It was my second adventure in a church. Not long before I was entombed for a night in an old chapel on an inaccessible mountain which was visited only once a year. It was an awful experience, but this one was worse. There was a wealthy lady in town, a good but pompous woman, who used to come to the church gorgeously painted up and attired with an enormous train and attendants. One Sunday I had just finished ringing the bell in the belfry and rushed downstairs when this grand dame was sweeping out and I jumped on her train. It tore off with a ripping noise which sounded like a salvo of musketry fired by raw recruits. My father was livid with rage. He gave me a gentle slap on the cheek, the only corporal punishment he ever administered to me but I almost feel it now. The embarrassment and confusion that followed are indescribable. I was practically ostracised until something else happened which redeemed me in the estimation of the community.

第二章 发明初体验
II. My First Efforts in Invention

叶窗看着窗外经过的陌生人。我生性腼腆,宁愿面对一头咆哮的狮子,也不愿面对一个四处溜达的城里人。但做礼拜才是我最难熬的考验,我得盛装出席布道会。在那里,我遇到了一场意外,时隔多年,一想到这件事,我仍心有余悸。那是我在教堂的第二次奇遇了。不久之前,我在一个古老的教堂里被困了一夜,那个小教堂在一座人迹罕至的山上,每年只对外开放一次。那是一次可怕的经历,但这一次,更糟糕。镇上有一位富有的女士,举止端庄但有点爱慕虚荣,每次来教堂都精心打扮,身穿带有长长裙裾的礼服。一个星期天,我在钟楼刚敲完钟,急匆匆下楼,这位女士拖着长长的裙摆也正好走过,我一脚踩上了她的裙裾,裙子发出撕裂的声音,听起来就像新兵们用火枪齐射一样。我父亲气得脸色发青,在我的脸上轻拍了一巴掌,这是他对我的唯一一次体罚,直到现在我还记忆犹新,随之而来的尴尬和窘迫无法形容。因为此事,我遭到了整个社区的排斥,直到发生了另一件事,才让我得到了救赎。

An enterprising young merchant had organized a fire department. A new fire engine was purchased, uniforms provided and the men drilled for service and parade. The engine was, in reality, a pump to be worked by sixteen men and was beautifully painted red and black. One afternoon the official trial was prepared for and the machine was transported to the river. The entire population turned out to witness the great spectacle. When all the speeches and ceremonies were concluded, the command was given to pump, but not a drop of water came from the nozzle. The professors and experts tried in vain to locate the trouble. The fizzle was complete when I arrived at the scene. My knowledge of the mechanism was nil and I knew next to nothing of air pressure, but instinctively I felt for the suction hose in the water and found that it had collapsed. When I waded in the river and opened it up the water rushed forth and not a few Sunday clothes were spoiled. Archimedes running naked through the streets of Syracuse and shouting Eureka at the top of his voice did not make a greater impression than myself. I was carried on the shoulders and was the hero of the day.

Upon settling in the city I began a four-year course in the so-called *Normal School* preparatory to my studies at the *College* or *Real Gymnasium*. During this period my boyish efforts and exploits, as well as troubles, continued. Among other things I attained the unique distinction of champion crow catcher in the country. My method of

第二章 发明初体验
II. My First Efforts in Invention

一个有进取心的年轻商人组建了一支消防队。他们购买了一套全新的消防器材，发放了制服，训练了消防员，准备进行检阅。实际上，这个消防器材就是一个抽水泵，被漆成了红黑相间的漂亮颜色，需要16个人协同操作。一天下午，检阅仪式准备就绪，机器被运到了河边，所有人都出来见证这一壮观的场面。当所有的致辞和仪式都结束后，抽水开始了，但喷嘴里没有出一滴水。教授和专家们试图找出问题所在，都徒劳无功。当我赶到现场时，故障还未排除。当时的我对机械知识一窍不通，对气压也一无所知，但出于本能，我摸了摸水中的吸水软管，发现它是瘪的。于是，我蹚水下河，打开了软管开关，水一下喷了出来，不少人的节日盛装都被淋湿了。我想，阿基米德在锡拉库萨的大街上裸奔，声嘶力竭地喊着"我发现了"，也不过如此了吧。我被众人扛在肩上，成了那天的英雄。

在戈斯皮奇定居后，我进入当地的预备学校开始了为期四年的学习，为以后我在专科或实科中学的学习打下了基础。在这期间，我少年时代的尝试、壮举，以及各种麻烦，还在继续。在众多殊荣当中，最值得说的是我获得过全国捕鸦冠军。我的方法非常简单，走进森林，躲在灌木丛中，模仿鸟的叫声，通

procedure was extremely simple. I would go in the forest, hide in the bushes, and imitate the call of the bird. Usually I would get several answers and in a short while a crow would flutter down into the shrubbery near me. After that all I needed to do was to throw a piece of cardboard to distract its attention, jump up and grab it before it could extricate itself from the undergrowth. In this way I would capture as many as I desired. But on one occasion something occurred which made me respect them. I had caught a fine pair of birds and was returning home with a friend. When we left the forest, thousands of crows had gathered making a frightful racket. In a few minutes they rose in pursuit and soon enveloped us. The fun lasted until all of a sudden I received a blow on the back of my head which knocked me down. Then they attacked me viciously. I was compelled to release the two birds and was glad to join my friend who had taken refuge in a cave.

In the schoolroom there were a few mechanical models which interested me and turned my attention to water turbines. I constructed many of these and found great pleasure in operating them. How extraordinary was my life an incident may illustrate. My uncle had no use for this kind of pastime and more than once rebuked me. I was fascinated by a description of Niagara Falls I had perused, and pictured in my imagination a big wheel run by the Falls. I told my uncle that I would go to America and carry out this scheme. Thirty years later I

第二章 发明初体验
II. My First Efforts in Invention

常我会得到几声回应，不一会儿，一只乌鸦就会飞到我附近的灌木丛里。之后，我需要做的就是扔一块纸板来分散它的注意力，在它飞离灌木丛之前跳起来抓住它。用这个办法，我想抓多少就能抓多少。但有一次发生的事情让我对它们肃然起敬。那次，我抓到了一对漂亮的鸟，和一个朋友一起准备回家。当我们离开森林时，数以千计的乌鸦聚集在一起，发出可怕的叫声。几分钟后，它们开始追赶我们，很快就把我们包围了。我开始还觉得很有趣，直到后脑勺遭到突然一击，我被击倒在地，接着，它们恶狠狠地攻击我。我不得不放了那两只鸟，逃到了朋友藏身的山洞里，躲过一难。

在学校的教室里，有几个机械模型让我爱不释手，并使我的注意力转向了水轮机。我建造了许多这样的模型，并在操作中得到了极大的乐趣。我的人生经历异于常人，在这里，试举一例。我的叔叔认为我这种消遣百无一用，不止一次地数落我。我曾认真研读过关于尼亚加拉大瀑布的介绍，并为之着迷，便在脑海中构建了一个由尼亚加拉瀑布驱动的巨型水轮机。我告诉叔叔我要去美国实施这个计划。30年后，见证自己的想法在尼亚加拉得以实现，我不禁惊叹于人类思想深不可测的奥秘。

63

saw my ideas carried out at Niagara and marveled at the unfathomable mystery of the mind.

I made all kinds of other contrivances and contraptions but among these the arbalists I produced were the best. My arrows, when shot, disappeared from sight and at close range traversed a plank of pine one inch thick. Through the continuous tightening of the bows I developed skin on my stomach very much like that of a crocodile and I am often wondering whether it is due to this exercise that I am able even now to digest cobble-stones! Nor can I pass in silence my performances with the sling which would have enabled me to give a stunning exhibit at the Hippodrome. And now I will tell of one of my feats with this antique implement of war which will strain to the utmost the credulity of the reader. I was practicing while walking with my uncle along the river. The sun was setting, the trout were playful and from time to time one would shoot up into the air, its glistening body sharply defined against a projecting rock beyond. Of course any boy might have hit a fish under these propitious conditions but I undertook a much more difficult task and I foretold to my uncle, to the minutest detail, what I intended doing. I was to hurl a stone to meet the fish, press its body against the rock, and cut it in two. It was no sooner said than done. My uncle looked at me almost scared out of his wits and exclaimed "Vade retro Satanas!" and it was a few days before he spoke to me again. Other records, however great, will be eclipsed but I feel that I could peacefully rest on my laurels for a thousand years.

第二章 发明初体验
II . My First Efforts in Invention

　　我制作了各种各样的设备和装置，但其中我做的箭弩是最好的。我的箭射出去，眨眼就消失不见，近距离内可以穿透一英寸厚的松木板。由于不断地拉弓，我练出了像鳄鱼皮一般紧实的腹肌。我经常在想，是不是因为这种锻炼，我的消化功能到现在都好得不得了呢！不得不提的还有我的绝技——抛掷，即使在古希腊竞技场也有我的一席之地。现在，我将讲述我使用这件古老的战争工具的一项壮举，读者们可不要惊掉下巴。一次，我一边练习，一边和叔叔在河边散步。夕阳西下，鳟鱼嬉戏，不时有一条蹿向空中，闪闪发光的鱼身在突出水面的岩石衬托下显得轮廓分明。在这种有利的条件下，任何男孩都有可能用石头击中一条鱼，但我挑战了一项更艰巨的任务，并告诉了叔叔我的详细计划。我打算扔一块石头，在鱼跳出水面的时候击中它，将它撞向岩石，使鱼身一分为二。不一会儿，我的计划就实现了！叔叔看着我，一脸惊愕，大喊道："撒旦！走开！"过了几天，他才敢和我说话。其他的纪录，不管多伟大，终会有人取而代之，但这个纪录，我觉得可以流传千古，无人能破。

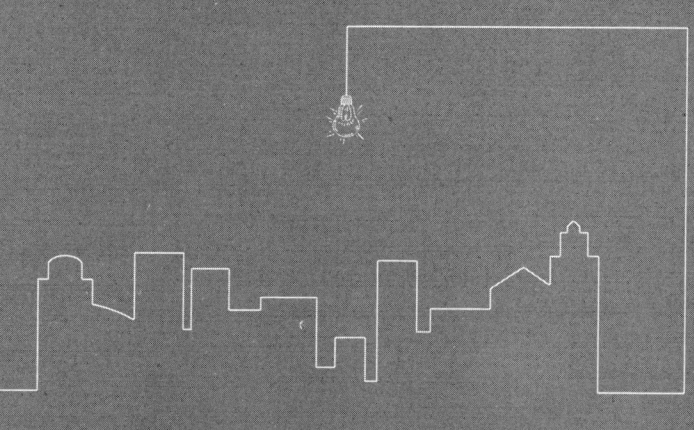

III. My Later Endeavors
第三章 后期诸尝试

At the age of ten I entered the Real Gymnasium which was a new and fairly well equipt institution. In the department of physics were various models of classical scientific apparatus, electrical and mechanical. The demonstrations and experiments performed from time to time by the instructors fascinated me and were undoubtedly a powerful incentive to invention. I was also passionately fond of mathematical studies and often won the professor's praise for rapid calculation. This was due to my acquired facility of visualizing the figures and performing the operations, not in the usual intuitive manner, but as in actual life. Up to a certain degree of complexity it was absolutely the same to me whether I wrote the symbols on the board or conjured them before my mental vision. But freehand drawing, to which many hours of the course were devoted, was an annoyance I could not endure. This was rather remarkable as most of the members of the family excelled in it. Perhaps my aversion was simply due to the predilection I found in undisturbed thought. Had it not been for a few exceptionally stupid boys, who could not do anything at all, my record would have been the worst. It was a serious handicap as under the then existing educational regime, drawing being obligatory, this deficiency threatened to spoil my whole career and my father had considerable trouble in railroading me from one class to another.

In the second year at that institution I became obsessed with

第三章 后期诸尝试
III. My Later Endeavors

  10岁时，我进入一所新建的实科中学上学，那里的设备相当完善。物理部有各种各样的经典科学仪器，有电子的，也有机械的。老师们时常进行的演示和实验让我着迷，这无疑是我从事发明的强大动力。我也热衷于数学研究，并经常因为运算快速赢得教授们的赞许。我拥有将数字具象化的天赋，然后不是靠直觉，而是像在实际生活中一样进行运算。就算复杂到一定程度，不管是把符号写在黑板上，还是在脑海中想象，对我来说，都是一样的。但是，我很厌恶手绘课，这门课程占据了大量的课时，让我难以忍受。说实话，这有点反常，因为家里大多数人在这方面都很出色。也许，我的厌恶仅仅是因为我偏爱不受干扰的思考。如果不是有几个特别笨的男孩，什么都不会，我的手绘成绩会垫底。这对我来说，是一个严重的阻碍，因为在当时的教育制度下，手绘是一门必修课，这方面的不足可能会毁掉我的整个职业生涯，我的父亲也是费了九牛二虎之力，逼着我去上每一节手绘课。

  在那所学校的第二年，我开始痴迷于通过稳定气压产生持

the idea of producing continuous motion through steady air pressure. The pump incident, of which I have told, had set afire my youthful imagination and imprest me with the boundless abilities of a vacuum. I grew frantic in my desire to harness this inexhaustible energy but for a long time I was groping in the dark. Finally, however, my endeavors crystallized in an invention which was to enable me to achieve what no other mortal ever attempted.

Imagine a cylinder freely rotatable on two bearings and partly surrounded by a rectangular trough which fits it perfectly. The open side of the trough is closed by a partition so that the cylindrical segment within the enclosure divides the latter into two compartments entirely separated from each other by air-tight sliding joints. One of these compartments being sealed and once for all exhausted, the other remaining open, a perpetual rotation of the cylinder would result, at least, I thought so. A wooden model was constructed and fitted with infinite care and when I applied the pump on one side and actually observed that there was a tendency to turning, I was delirious with joy. Mechanical flight was the one thing I wanted to accomplish although still under the discouraging recollection of a bad fall I sustained by jumping with an umbrella from the top of a building. Every day I used to transport myself through the air to distant regions but could not understand just how I managed to do it. Now I had something concrete—

续动能的想法。前面说过的水泵事件点燃了我旺盛的想象力，让我对真空的无限能量印象深刻。我疯狂渴望能驾驭这种取之不尽用之不竭的能量，但很长一段时间里，我都是在黑暗中摸索。最终，一项发明诞生了，这项发明是我努力的结晶，让我实现了前无古人的创举。

想象一下，有一根轴，两端各安一个轴承，轴可自由旋转，且部分被一个矩形凹槽所包围。矩形凹槽与轴完美契合，开口侧用隔离板密封，形成一个密闭空间，并且这个空间被轴分成两个隔间。这俩隔间由相当于气密滑动接头的轴完全分离，其中一个隔间保持密封，将其内部空气一次抽空，而另一个隔间保持敞开，这样，轴就可以不停旋转，至少，我是这么认为的。于是，我小心翼翼地组装了一个木制模型，并在模型一侧装了个抽气泵。当确实观察到木轴有转动的趋势时，我欣喜若狂。机械飞行是我一直想完成的一件事，当年我撑着伞，从楼顶纵身一跃，结果摔个半死，这件事到现在我仍记忆犹新。每天我都想象着自己可以飞到遥远的地方，但如何才能做到，却一直没有思路。现在，我有了些具体的想法——做一架飞行器，只要有旋转的轴、扇动的机翼和拥有无限能量的真空体，足矣！从那时起，我想象着每天乘坐舒适豪华的飞行器到各地旅行，就像所罗门国王和他的飞毯一样。不过，多年以后我才明白，

a flying machine with nothing more than a rotating shaft, flapping wings, and—a vacuum of unlimited power! From that time on I made my daily aerial excursions in a vehicle of comfort and luxury as might have befitted King Solomon. It took years before I understood that the atmospheric pressure acted at right angles to the surface of the cylinder and that the slight rotary effort I observed was due to a leak. Though this knowledge came gradually it gave me a painful shock.

I had hardly completed my course at the Real Gymnasium when I was prostrated with a dangerous illness or rather, a score of them, and my condition became so desperate that I was given up by physicians. During this period I was permitted to read constantly, obtaining books from the Public Library which had been neglected and entrusted to me for classification of the works and preparation of the catalogues. One day I was handed a few volumes of new literature unlike anything I had ever read before and so captivating as to make me utterly forget my hopeless state. They were the earlier works of Mark Twain and to them might have been due the miraculous recovery which followed. Twenty-five years later, when I met Mr. Clemens and we formed a friendship between us, I told him of the experience and was amazed to see that great man of laughter burst into tears.

因为气压垂直作用于木轴表面，我观察到的轻微转动不过是漏气导致。虽然是逐渐知道这一点的，但我还是备受打击。

我还没在学校念完书，就被一种可怕的疾病，或者更确切地说，是被几十种疾病压倒了。我的身体状况十分糟糕，医生都觉得我没救了。在此期间，我获准可以阅读，于是从公共图书馆借阅各种书籍，那时的图书馆总是无人问津，便委托我对藏书进行分类、编制目录。有一天，我得到了几本新的文学作品，与我以往读过的任何一本都不同，十分引人入胜，让我彻底忘了自己的绝望境地。这几本书，都是马克·吐温的早期作品，也许正是因为它们，我才奇迹般康复了。25年后，我遇到克莱门斯①先生本人并与他成为好友。有一次，我向他讲述了这段经历，惊讶地看到这位伟大的幽默大师突然泪流满面。

---

① 马克·吐温原名萨缪尔·兰亨·克莱门斯。——译者注

My studies were continued at the higher *Real Gymnasium* in Carlstadt, Croatia, where one of my aunts resided. She was a distinguished lady, the wife of a Colonel who was an old warhorse having participated in many battles. I never can forget the three years I passed at their home. No fortress in time of war was under a more rigid discipline. I was fed like a canary bird. All the meals were of the highest quality and deliciously prepared but short in quantity by a thousand percent. The slices of ham cut by my aunt were like tissue paper. When the Colonel would put something substantial on my plate she would snatch it away and say excitedly to him: "Be careful, Niko is very delicate." I had a voracious appetite and suffered like Tantalus. But I lived in an atmosphere of refinement and artistic taste quite unusual for those times and conditions. The land was low and marshy and malaria fever never left me while there despite of the enormous amounts of quinin I consumed. Occasionally the river would rise and drive an army of rats into the buildings, devouring everything even to the bundles of the fierce paprika. These pests were to me a welcome diversion. I thinned their ranks by all sorts of means, which won me the unenviable distinction of rat-catcher in the community. At last, however, my course was completed, the misery ended, and I obtained the certificate of maturity which brought me to the cross-roads.

第三章 后期诸尝试
III. My Later Endeavors

后来，我去了克罗地亚，在卡尔施塔特的一所实科高中继续学习。我有一个姑妈住在那里，她是一位尊贵的女士，丈夫是一位身经百战的上校。在他们家度过的三年时光，我永生难忘。他们家的纪律，跟战争时期任何一座堡垒的相比，都毫不逊色。我就像一只金丝雀一样被喂养着，每一餐都很讲究食材，而且美味可口，但分量却少之又少。姑妈切的火腿片薄得像张纸。每当姑父给我多夹点菜时，她都会一把抢过去，激动地对他说："小心点，尼科①的身子很弱的。"我其实胃口很好，却每天面对美味佳肴而不能吃，挨饥受饿像坦塔罗斯②一样痛苦。但总体而言，我当时的生活充满了高雅和精致的艺术氛围，这点与当下的环境不太一样。那里地势低洼，沼泽遍布，尽管我服用了大量的奎宁，但疟疾从未离开过我。偶尔河水会上涨，把老鼠大军赶到房子里，它们什么都啃，连一包包浓烈的辣椒粉也不放过。这些有害的动物，对我来说却是一种消遣，我使出各种手段削弱了它们的队伍，这为我在社区中赢得了"捕鼠达人"这一尴尬头衔。终于，学业完成了，痛苦结束了，我也成年了，来到了人生的十字路口。

---

① 尼古拉·特斯拉的昵称。
② 古希腊神话中宙斯之子，因罪恶滔天被打入地狱。被囚禁在深水池中，喝不到水也吃不到果实。——译者注

During all those years my parents never wavered in their resolve to make me embrace the clergy, the mere thought of which filled me with dread. I had become intensely interested in electricity under the stimulating influence of my Professor of Physics, who was an ingenious man and often demonstrated the principles by apparatus of his own invention. Among these I recall a device in the shape of a freely rotatable bulb, with tinfoil coatings, which was made to spin rapidly when connected to a static machine. It is impossible for me to convey an adequate idea of the intensity of feeling I experienced in witnessing his exhibitions of these mysterious phenomena. Every impression produced a thousand echoes in my mind. I wanted to know more of this wonderful force; I longed for experiment and investigation and resigned myself to the inevitable with aching heart.

Just as I was making ready for the long journey home I received word that my father wished me to go on a shooting expedition. It was a strange request as he had been always strenuously opposed to this kind of sport. But a few days later I learned that the cholera was raging in that district and, taking advantage of an opportunity, I returned to Gospic in disregard of my parents' wishes. It is incredible how absolutely ignorant people were as to the causes of this scourge which visited the country in intervals of from fifteen to twenty years. They thought that the deadly agents were transmitted through the air and filled it with pungent odors

这些年来，我的父母一直坚定地想让我效力于教会，但我志不在此，每每念及此事就心生厌恶。在我的物理老师的影响下，我对电学产生了浓厚的兴趣。他是一个富有创造力的人，经常用自己发明的仪器演示电学原理。在这些仪器中，我记得有个装置，是一个可以自由旋转的灯泡，上面裹了一层锡箔纸，当连接到静电起电机时，就会快速旋转。目睹他演示的这些神秘现象，我深受震撼，激动之情难以言表，脑子里也是千头万绪，久久不能平静。我想更深入地了解这种奇妙的力量，我渴望进行实验和调查，却不得不屈从于父母的安排，心如刀割。

正当我准备长途跋涉回家时，我却收到父亲的消息，希望我去参加一个射击比赛。这很奇怪，因为他一直极力反对这种运动。几天后，我才得知，是因为家乡霍乱肆虐，但当时正好有个返乡的机会，于是我不顾父母的意愿，回到了戈斯皮奇。令人难以置信的是，对于这种每隔15年至20年就发一次的瘟疫的起因，当时的人们竟然一无所知。他们认为，这些致命的病毒是通过空气传播的，于是不断地喷洒消毒水，焚烧秸秆，空气中弥漫着刺鼻的气味和烟雾。与此同时，他们却继续饮用被

and smoke. In the meantime they drank the infected water and died in heaps. I contracted the awful disease on the very day of my arrival and although surviving the crisis, I was confined to bed for nine months with scarcely any ability to move. My energy was completely exhausted and for the second time I found myself at death's door. In one of the sinking spells which was thought to be the last, my father rushed into the room. I still see his pallid face as he tried to cheer me in tones belying his assurance. "Perhaps," I said, "I may get well if you will let me study engineering." "You will go to the best technical institution in the world," he solemnly replied, and I knew that he meant it. A heavy weight was lifted from my mind but the relief would have come too late had it not been for a marvelous cure brought about through a bitter decoction of a peculiar bean. I came to life like another Lazarus to the utter amazement of everybody.

My father insisted that I spend a year in healthful physical outdoor exercises to which I reluctantly consented. For most of this term I roamed in the mountains, loaded with a hunter's outfit and a bundle of books, and this contact with nature made me stronger in body as well as in mind. I thought and planned, and conceived many ideas almost as a rule delusive. The vision was clear enough but the knowledge of principles was very limited. In one of my inventions I proposed to convey letters and packages across the seas, through a submarine tube,

污染的水,接二连三地死去。我在抵达的当天就染上了这种可怕的疾病,虽然最终挺过了这场危机,但却在床上躺了整整九个月,一动也不能动,精力也消耗殆尽,生平第二次命悬一线。有一天,我感觉自己真的快要死了,当时父亲冲进房间,我至今还记得他脸色苍白,故作镇定为我打气。"也许,"我说,"如果你让我学工程的话,我可能会好起来。""你会去世界上最好的工学院。"他郑重地回答。我知道他是认真的,心中的重担一下子卸了下来,加上用一种奇特的豆子熬制的苦汤起到了神奇的疗效,这一切来得还不太晚。我像《圣经》中的拉撒路[①]一样奇迹般活了过来,让所有人都惊讶不已。

接下来整整一年,父亲要求我进行户外锻炼,说有益健康,我勉强同意了。绝大部分时间里,我一身猎人行头,背着一捆书,在山间漫步,置身山水对我的身心裨益良多。我思考、计划并构思了许多几乎是妄想的想法。我的思路足够清晰,但对原理的了解却很有限。我在一项发明中,提议通过海底管道,将信件和包裹装在强度足以抵抗液压的球形容器中,

---

① 拉撒路,《圣经》中记载的人物,他病死后耶稣断定他可以复活,而他真的在死后四天复活,证明了耶稣的神迹。

in spherical containers of sufficient strength to resist the hydraulic pressure. The pumping plant, intended to force the water through the tube, was accurately figured and designed and all other particulars carefully worked out. Only one trifling detail, of no consequence, was lightly dismissed. I assumed an arbitrary velocity of the water and, what is more, took pleasure in making it high, thus arriving at a stupendous performance supported by faultless calculations. Subsequent reflections, however, on the resistance of pipes to fluid flow determined me to make this invention public property.

Another one of my projects was to construct a ring around the equator which would, of course, float freely and could be arrested in its spinning motion by reactionary forces, thus enabling travel at a rate of about one thousand miles an hour, impracticable by rail. The reader will smile. The plan was difficult of execution, I will admit, but not nearly so bad as that of a well-known New York professor, who wanted to pump the air from the torrid to the temperate zones, entirely forgetful of the fact that the Lord had provided a gigantic machine for this very purpose.

Still another scheme, far more important and attractive, was to derive power from the rotational energy of terrestrial bodies. I had discovered that objects on the earth's surface, owing to the diurnal rotation of the globe, are carried by the same alternately in and against

送达大洋彼岸。为了驱动管道内的水流动，我通过精确计算，设计了一个泵站，包括所有细节的制定，只有一个无关紧要的小细节被忽略了。我很武断地假定了一个水速，而且，我喜欢把它定得很高，从而在完美的计算支持下得出了一个惊人的性能。但是，后来考虑到管壁对水流阻力的因素，我决定将这项发明无偿共享。

我的另一个设想是在赤道周围建造一个环形轨道。当然，这个轨道可以自由悬浮，并通过反作用力阻止其自转，从而使旅行的速度达到每小时约1000英里，这是铁路无法实现的。看到这，读者可能会付诸一笑。我承认，这个计划执行起来很困难，但远不及纽约一位知名教授的计划那么糟糕，他想把热带地区的空气输送到温带，全然忘记了上帝早已为此提供了一台庞大的机器。

我还有一个更重要更具吸引力的方案，就是从地球自转中获取动力。我发现，由于地球的自转，地球表面的物体会交替地受到沿相同或相反方向的平移推力，由此产生巨大的动量变化，可以用最简单的方式为世界上任何可居住地区提供动力。

the direction of translatory movement. From this results a great change in momentum which could be utilized in the simplest imaginable manner to furnish motive effort in any habitable region of the world. I cannot find words to describe my disappointment when later I realized that I was in the predicament of Archimedes, who vainly sought for a fixed point in the universe.

At the termination of my vacation I was sent to the *Polytechnic School in Gratz*, Styria, which my father had chosen as one of the oldest and best reputed institutions. That was the moment I had eagerly awaited and I began my studies under good auspices and firmly resolved to succeed. My previous training was above the average, due to my father's teaching and opportunities afforded. I had acquired the knowledge of a number of languages and waded through the books of several libraries, picking up information more or less useful. Then again, for the first time, I could choose my subjects as I liked, and free-hand drawing was to bother me no more.

I had made up my mind to give my parents a surprise, and during the whole first year I regularly started my work at three o'clock in the morning and continued until eleven at night, no Sundays or holidays excepted. As most of my fellow-students took thinks easily, naturally enough I eclipsed all records. In the course of that year I past through

第三章 后期诸尝试
III. My Later Endeavors

可是后来我意识到自己陷入了阿基米德的困境,就像他妄想在宇宙中寻找一个支点一样,我无法用言语来形容我的失望之情。

假期结束后,我被送到了斯蒂里亚的格拉茨理工学院,它是最古老、声誉最好的学校之一,父亲为我精心挑选的学校。这是我热切期盼的时刻,万事俱备,我开始了我的学业,并决心要做出一番成就。由于父亲的教导和之前的训练,我的水平要高于一般同学。在那时我已经掌握了多种语言,翻阅了好几个图书馆的书籍后,或多或少学到了一些有用的知识。而且,平生第一次我可以随心所欲地选择我喜欢的课程,不用再受手绘课的折磨了。

我下定决心要给父母一个惊喜,在整个第一年里,我凌晨三点开始学习,一直到晚上十一点,没有周末或假日。由于大多数同学都学得不求甚解,我自然打破了各项成绩纪录。在那一年里,我以满分的成绩通过了九门考试,而且教授们认为满分还不能完全代表我的真实水平。带着一大摞奖状证书,我回

nine exams and the professors thought I deserved more than the highest qualifications. Armed with their flattering certificates, I went home for a short rest, expecting a triumph, and was mortified when my father made light of these hard won honors. That almost killed my ambition; but later, after he had died, I was pained to find a package of letters which the professors had written him to the effect that unless he took me away from the Institution I would be killed through overwork.

Thereafter I devoted myself chiefly to physics, mechanics and mathematical studies, spending the hours of leisure in the libraries. I had a veritable mania for finishing whatever I began, which often got me into difficulties. On one occasion I started to read the works of Voltaire when I learned, to my dismay, that there were close on one hundred large volumes in small print which that monster had written while drinking seventy-two cups of black coffee per diem. It had to be done, but when I laid aside the last book I was very glad, and said, "Never more!"

My first year's showing had won me the appreciation and friendship of several professors. Among these were Prof. Rogner, who was teaching arithmetical subjects and geometry; Prof. Poeschl, who held the chair of theoretical and experimental physics, and Dr. Allé, who taught integral calculus and specialized in differential equations.

家了,打算休整几日,并期待着父母感受我胜利的喜悦,可父亲对这些来之不易的荣誉竟然不屑一顾,我崩溃了,这几乎扼杀了我的雄心壮志。但后来,在他去世后,我发现了教授们写给他的一包信件,大意是如果他再不把我从学院带走,我可能会因过劳而死,得知这一切我悲痛难抑。

自那以后,我主要致力于物理、机械学和数学研究,闲暇时间都泡在图书馆。我这个人,非常执拗,一旦开始做什么,就必须得完成,这常常让我陷入困境。有一次,我开始阅读伏尔泰的作品,结果沮丧地发现,那个怪物每天喝72杯黑咖啡,写成了这近一百卷小字印刷的大块头。但开弓没有回头箭,当我合上最后一卷时,长舒了一口气:"再也不读了!"

我第一年的表现赢得了几位教授的赞赏,我们也成了朋友。其中包括教授算术和几何学的罗格纳教授、担任理论和实验物理学课程的波施尔教授,以及教授微积分和专门研究微分方程的阿勒博士——这位科学家是我接触过的最出色的讲师,对我特别关照,经常会在教室里待上一两个小时为我答疑解惑。我

This scientist was the most brilliant lecturer to whom I ever listened. He took a special interest in my progress and would frequently remain for an hour or two in the lecture room, giving me problems to solve, in which I delighted. To him I explained a flying machine I had conceived, not an illusionary invention, but one based on sound, scientific principles, which has become realizable through my turbine and will soon be given to the world. Both Professors Rogner and Poeschl were curious men. The former had peculiar ways of expressing himself and whenever he did so there was a riot, followed by a long and embarrassing pause. Prof. Poeschl was a methodical and thoroughly grounded German. He had enormous feet and hands like the paws of a bear, but all of his experiments were skillfully performed with lock-like precision and without a miss.

It was in the second year of my studies that we received a Gramme dynamo from Paris, having the horseshoe form of a laminated field magnet, and a wire-wound armature with a commutator. It was connected up and various effects of the currents were shown. While Prof. Poeschl was making demonstrations, running the machine as a motor, the brushes gave trouble, sparking badly, and I observed that it might be possible to operate a motor without these appliances. But he declared that it could not be done and did me the honor of delivering a lecture on the subject, at the conclusion of which he remarked:

第三章 后期诸尝试
III. My Later Endeavors

也乐在其中。我向他介绍了我构思的飞行器，这不是一个幻想，而是一个基于合理科学原理的发明，通过我制作的涡轮机可以实现，并将很快问世。罗格纳教授和波施尔教授都是很古怪的人。前者有着独特的表达方式，每当他发表什么言论，都会引起一些骚动，接着是漫长而尴尬的停顿。而后者则是一个有条不紊、脚踏实地的德国人，他的手脚大如熊掌，但做起实验来，每次都驾轻就熟，分毫不差。

在我学习的第二年，我们收到了一台来自巴黎的格拉姆发电机，它有着马蹄形的层状磁场，以及一个带有换向器的绕线电枢，连上电会产生各种电流效应。当波施尔教授将机器作为电机运行时，电刷出现了故障，火花四溅，我认为没有这些设备也可以运行电机，但他宣称这是不可能的，并就这一问题发表了演讲，在演讲结束时他说："特斯拉先生可能会取得伟大的成就，但在这一点上他肯定永远也做不到。这相当于把一个稳定的拉力，如重力，转换成一个旋转的力。这是一个永动机计划，一个不可能实现的想法。"但直觉是超越知识的东西。毫无

"Mr. Tesla may accomplish great things, but he certainly never will do this. It would be equivalent to converting a steadily pulling force, like that of gravity, into a rotary effort. It is a perpetual motion scheme, an impossible idea." But instinct is something which transcends knowledge. We have, undoubtedly, certain finer fibers that enable us to perceive truths when logical deduction, or any other willful effort of the brain, is futile. For a time I wavered, imprest by the professor's authority, but soon became convinced I was right and undertook the task with all the fire and boundless confidence of youth.

I started by first picturing in my mind a direct-current machine, running it and following the changing flow of the currents in the armature. Then I would imagine an alternator and investigate the processes taking place in a similar manner. Next I would visualize systems comprising motors and generators and operate them in various ways. The images I saw were to me perfectly real and tangible. All my remaining term in Gratz was passed in intense but fruitless efforts of this kind, and I almost came to the conclusion that the problem was insolvable.

In 1880 I went to Prague, Bohemia, carrying out my father's wish to complete my education at the University there. It was in that city that I made a decided advance, which consisted in detaching the

疑问，我们有某种更精细的神经纤维，使我们能够在逻辑推理或大脑的主观意志都失效的情况下感知真理。有一段时间，因为教授的权威，我动摇了，但很快就坚信自己是对的，我满怀信心、豪情万丈地启动了这项任务。

首先，我在脑海中想象一台直流发电机，启动它，并追踪电枢中电流的变化。然后，我会想象一台交流发电机，并以类似的方式研究其变化。接下来，我又想象出由电机和发电机组成的系统，并以各种方式运行它们。我看到的图像对我来说是完全真实和有形的。我在格拉茨理工学院的所有剩余时光都是在这种紧张但徒劳的努力中度过的，我几乎可以得出结论，这个问题无法解决。

1880年，我去了波西米亚的布拉格，准备实现父亲的愿望，在布拉格大学完成学业。正是在那座城市，我取得了决定性的进展。我把换向器从机器上拆下来，看有无新的变化，但

commutator from the machine and studying the phenomena in this new aspect, but still without result. In the year following there was a sudden change in my views of life. I realized that my parents had been making too great sacrifices on my account and resolved to relieve them of the burden. The wave of the American telephone had just reached the European continent and the system was to be installed in Budapest, Hungary. It appeared an ideal opportunity, all the more as a friend of our family was at the head of the enterprise. It was here that I suffered the complete breakdown of the nerves to which I have referred.

What I experienced during the period of that illness surpasses all belief. My sight and hearing were always extraordinary. I could clearly discern objects in the distance when others saw no trace of them. Several times in my boyhood I saved the houses of our neighbors from fire by hearing the faint crackling sounds which did not disturb their sleep, and calling for help.

In 1899, when I was past forty and carrying on my experiments in Colorado, I could hear very distinctly thunderclaps at a distance of 550 miles. The limit of audition for my young assistants was scarcely more than 150 miles. My ear was thus over thirteen times more sensitive. Yet at that time I was, so to speak, stone deaf in comparison with the acuteness of my hearing while under the nervous strain. In Budapest I

第三章 后期诸尝试
III. My Later Endeavors

仍无结果。在接下来的一年里，我对生活的看法发生了突变。我意识到，我的父母为我做出了太大的牺牲，于是决心减轻他们的负担。美国的电话机热潮刚刚抵达欧洲大陆，匈牙利的布达佩斯准备安装通话系统，这似乎是一个理想的机会，更何况我们家的一个朋友是这个企业的负责人。但正是此时，我遭受了之前所提到的精神完全崩溃的痛苦。

我在患病期间的那段经历超出了我所有的想象。我的视力和听力一向很好，我能清楚地分辨出远处别人看不见的物体。在童年时代，有好几次我听到了邻居的房子发出微弱的噼啪声，可他们在睡梦中并没有察觉，于是我大声呼救，才使他们免受火灾。

1899年，当我年过四旬，在科罗拉多州做实验时，我可以非常清楚地听到550英里以外的雷鸣声，而我的年轻助手们的听觉极限几乎不超过150英里。我的耳朵比别人敏感13倍以上。但即便如此，那个时候的我，与我在神经紧张情况下的听力敏锐程度相比，完全是个聋子。在布达佩斯，我可以听到三个房间外手表的嘀嗒声；一只苍蝇落在房间的桌子上，都会在

91

could hear the ticking of a watch with three rooms between me and the time-piece. A fly alighting on a table in the room would cause a dull thud in my ear. A carriage passing at a distance of a few miles fairly shook my whole body. The whistle of a locomotive twenty or thirty miles away made the bench or chair on which I sat vibrate so strongly that the pain was unbearable. The ground under my feet trembled continuously. I had to support my bed on rubber cushions to get any rest at all. The roaring noises from near and far often produced the effect of spoken words which would have frightened me had I not been able to resolve them into their accidental components. The sun's rays, when periodically intercepted, would cause blows of such force on my brain that they would stun me. I had to summon all my will power to pass under a bridge or other structure as I experienced a crushing pressure on the skull. In the dark I had the sense of a bat and could detect the presence of an object at a distance of twelve feet by a peculiar creepy sensation on the forehead. My pulse varied from a few to two hundred and sixty beats and all the tissues of the body quivered with twitchings and tremors which was perhaps the hardest to bear. A renowned physician who gave me daily large doses of Bromide of Potassium pronounced my malady unique and incurable.

It is my eternal regret that I was not under the observation of experts in physiology and psychology at that time. I clung desperately to

第三章 后期诸尝试
III. My Later Endeavors

我耳边发出沉闷的砰的一声；一辆马车在几英里远的地方驶过，都会震得我全身发抖；二三十英里外火车头的汽笛声都能让我坐的长凳或椅子剧烈震动，痛苦不堪。我脚下的地面也不停地颤抖，不得不将橡胶垫子铺在床下，才能得到片刻安宁。这些或远或近的轰鸣声就像有人在我耳边低语，要不是我能辨出缘由，一定经常会被吓得不轻；太阳光照在我头上，对我的大脑会造成强烈冲击，使我头晕目眩；当我从桥梁或其他建筑物下面通过时，我得调动所有的意志力，才能对抗可以碾碎头骨的压力；在黑暗中，我就像是一只蝙蝠，可以通过前额一种令人发寒的奇特感觉，探测到12英尺远的物体存在；我的脉搏从几下到260下不等，身体的所有组织都随之抽搐和颤抖，这或许是最难以忍受的。一位知名医生每天给我大剂量的溴化钾，并断定我的病十分罕见，无法治愈。

当时没有接受生理学和心理学专家的观察，这是我永远的遗憾。我拼了命地抓住生命的衣袖，但从未想过有一天会守得

life, but never expected to recover. Can anyone believe that so hopeless a physical wreck could ever be transformed into a man of astonishing strength and tenacity, able to work thirty-eight years almost without a day's interruption, and find himself still strong and fresh in body and mind? Such is my case. A powerful desire to live and to continue the work, and the assistance of a devoted friend and athlete accomplished the wonder. My health returned and with it the vigor of mind. In attacking the problem again I almost regretted that the struggle was soon to end. I had so much energy to spare. When I undertook the task it was not with a resolve such as men often make. With me it was a sacred vow, a question of life and death. I knew that I would perish if I failed. Now I felt that the battle was won. Back in the deep recesses of the brain was the solution, but I could not yet give it outward expression. One afternoon, which is ever present in my recollection, I was enjoying a walk with my friend in the City Park and reciting poetry. At that age I knew entire books by heart, word for word. One of these was Goethe's Faust. The sun was just setting and reminded me of the glorious passage:

"Sie rückt und weicht, der Tag ist überlebt, Dort eilt sie hin und fördert neues Leben. Oh, dass kein Flügel mich vom Boden hebt, Ihr nach und immer nach zu streben!

第三章 后期诸尝试
III. My Later Endeavors

云开见月明。谁能相信,如此无望的一个破败身躯,竟然能变得如此力量惊人,韧性十足,能够几乎不间断地工作38年,身心仍然鲜活有力呢?我做到了!靠着对生活和继续工作的强烈渴望,在一位挚友兼运动达人的帮助下,我创造了这一奇迹,恢复了身体健康,也恢复了思想活力。再次思考之前的旋转磁场难题,我甚至有点惋惜,这场战役将很快宣告结束。我有用不完的精力,面对这项挑战时,我的决心与常人不同。对我来说,这是一个神圣的誓言,事关生死。我知道,如果我失败了,我就会死亡。现在,我觉得这场战斗胜利在望了。答案就藏在我大脑深处,只是我还不知道如何表达。有一天下午,我和我的朋友在城市公园里一边散步,一边朗诵诗歌,这个场景一直深深印在我的记忆中。在那个年纪,我能用心记住整本书,一字不差。其中有本书是歌德的《浮士德》。当时,夕阳西沉,我想起了那段脍炙人口的诗句:

Ein schöner Traum indessen sie entweicht, Ach, zu des Geistes Flügeln wird so leicht Kein körperlicher Flügel sich gesellen!"

[The glow retreats, done is the day of toil; It yonder hastes, new fields of life exploring; Ah, that no wing can lift me from the soil Upon its track to follow, follow soaring!

A glorious dream! though now the glories fade. Alas! the wings that lift the mind no aid. Of wings to lift the body can bequeath me.]

As I uttered these inspiring words the idea came like a flash of lightning and in an instant the truth was revealed. I drew with a stick on the sand the diagrams shown six years later in my address before the American Institute of Electrical Engineers, and my companion understood them perfectly. The images I saw were wonderfully sharp and clear and had the solidity of metal and stone, so much so that I told him: "See my motor here; watch me reverse it." I cannot begin to describe my emotions. Pygmalion seeing his statue come to life could not have been more deeply moved. A thousand secrets of nature which I might have stumbled upon accidentally I would have given for that one which I had wrested from her against all odds and at the peril of my existence.

第三章 后期诸尝试
III. My Later Endeavors

> 日落西山苦役终，心有猛虎叹匆匆。
> 只恨身无振飞翼，追随理想向天冲。

> 我欲上天揽明月，奈何梦醒北风中。
> 理想之花多绚烂，身如残烛一场空。

当我念出这些振奋人心的句子时，灵光一现，一个想法蹦了出来，真相在这一瞬间显露出来。我找到一根棍子，在沙地上画出了示意图，这些简图，与六年后我在美国电气工程师协会作报告时一模一样，我的那位朋友也完全看懂了。我看到的图像非常清晰明朗，有板有眼，我告诉他："看，我的马达在这里，看我把它倒过来。"我的激动之情难以言表，也许，皮格马利翁①看到他雕刻的塑像活了过来，也不过如此吧。也许机缘巧合，我曾窥见自然界的一千个秘密，但我也愿意用它们来换取这个发现，毕竟这是我不顾一切，赌上了身家性命从大自然手中夺来的。

---

① 希腊神话中的塞浦路斯国王，擅长雕刻。

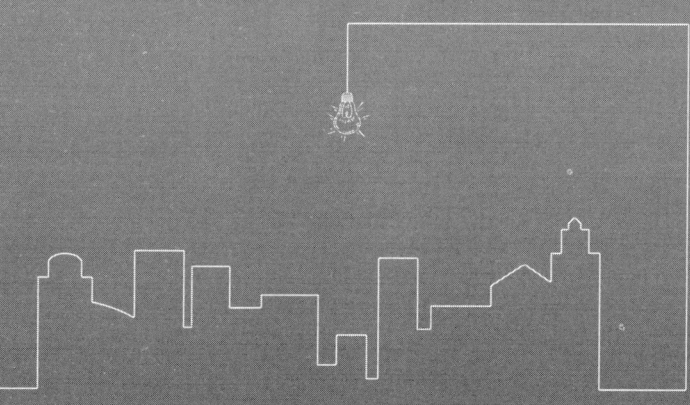

IV. The Discovery of the Tesla Coil and Transformer
第四章 特斯拉线圈和变压器的发现

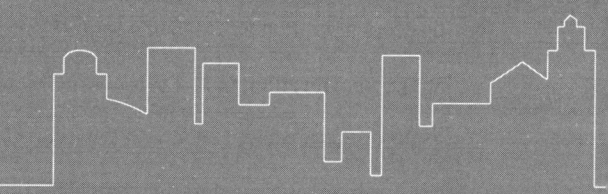

For a while I gave myself up entirely to the intense enjoyment of picturing machines and devising new forms. It was a mental state of happiness about as complete as I have ever known in life. Ideas came in an uninterrupted stream and the only difficulty I had was to hold them fast. The pieces of apparatus I conceived were to me absolutely real and tangible in every detail, even to the minute marks and signs of wear. I delighted in imagining the motors constantly running, for in this way they presented to mind's eye a more fascinating sight. When natural inclination develops into a passionate desire, one advances towards his goal in seven-league boots. In less than two months I evolved virtually all the types of motors and modifications of the system which are now identified with my name. It was, perhaps, providential that the necessities of existence commanded a temporary halt to this consuming activity of the mind. I came to Budapest prompted by a premature report concerning the telephone enterprise and, as irony of fate willed it, I had to accept a position as draftsman in the Central Telegraph Office of the Hungarian Government at a salary which I deem it my privilege not to disclose! Fortunately, I soon won the interest of the Inspector-in-Chief and was thereafter employed on calculations, designs and estimates in connection with new installations, until the Telephone Exchange was started, when I took charge of the same. The knowledge and practical experience I gained in the course of this work was most valuable and

第四章 特斯拉线圈和变压器的发现
IV. The Discovery of the Tesla Coil and Transformer

有一段时间，我完全沉浸在绘制机器和设计新机型的极致享受中，那种精神层次的幸福感，铺天盖地，无可比拟。灵感源源不断地涌现，我唯一的困难是如何迅速把它们抓住。对我来说，我构思的每一块设备部件都绝对真实，每一个细节都有迹可循，甚至包括一些细微的磨损痕迹。我开心地想象着电机在不停运转，在脑海中呈现出更加迷人的景象。当个人的偏好发展成一种强烈的欲望时，他就如同脚踏风火轮，朝着目标飞速前进。在不到两个月的时间里，我几乎研发出了所有类型的电机，并对以我名字命名的电机系统进行了改进。也许是天意，生存的需要让我暂时停止了这种耗费脑力的活动。在电话公司一份早期报告的催促下，我来到了布达佩斯，讽刺的是，我不得不接受匈牙利政府提供的一份工作——中央电报局绘图员，关于工资嘛，打死我也不会透露的！但幸运的是，我很快就赢得了局长的赏识，此后，我受雇于负责新装置有关的计算、设计和评估工作，直到电话交换机出现，我又负责类似的相关工作。在这项工作中，我获得的知识和实践经验弥足珍贵，有大量的机会锻炼我的发明能力。我对中央车站的设备做了一些升级，并对电话中继器或放大器进行了完善，这个虽然从未申请专利，也未在任何公开场合提及，但就算放到今天，也得感谢我的功劳。我的工作效率如此之高，这个项目的负责人普斯卡斯先生，在处理完布达佩斯的业务后，为我提供了一份在巴黎的工作，我欣然接受了。

the employment gave me ample opportunities for the exercise of my inventive faculties. I made several improvements in the Central Station apparatus and perfected a telephone repeater or amplifier which was never patented or publicly described but would be creditable to me even today. In recognition of my efficient assistance the organizer of the undertaking, Mr. Puskas, upon disposing of his business in Budapest, offered me a position in Paris which I gladly accepted.

I never can forget the deep impression that magic city produced on my mind. For several days after my arrival I roamed through the streets in utter bewilderment of the new spectacle. The attractions were many and irresistible, but, alas, the income was spent as soon as received. When Mr. Puskas asked me how I was getting along in the new sphere, I described the situation accurately in the statement that "the last twenty-nine days of the month are the toughest"! I led a rather strenuous life in what would now be termed "Rooseveltian fashion". Every morning, regardless of weather, I would go from the Boulevard St. Marcel, where I resided, to a bathing house on the Seine, plunge into the water, loop the circuit twenty-seven times and then walk an hour to reach Ivry, where the Company's factory was located. There I would have a woodchopper's breakfast at half-past seven o'clock and then eagerly await the lunch hour, in the meanwhile cracking hard nuts for the Manager of the Works, Mr. Charles Batchellor, who was an intimate

第四章 特斯拉线圈和变压器的发现
IV. The Discovery of the Tesla Coil and Transformer

我永远也忘不了巴黎这座梦幻之城在我心中留下的深刻印象。在到达后的几天里,我每天都在街上游荡,被眼前的花花世界迷了眼。这座城市吸引人的地方很多,都令人无法抗拒,唉,薪水一到手就花光了。当普斯卡斯先生问我在巴黎过得如何时,我准确地形容了我的情况:"每个月的最后29天是最艰难的!"我过的日子非常有规律,现在的人把它叫作"罗斯福式生活",每天早晨,无论天气如何,我都会从我居住的圣马塞尔大道出发,到达塞纳河畔的一家游泳场,跳进泳池,游上27圈,然后,再步行一小时到达公司工厂所在地伊夫里。七点半,我在那吃完简易早餐,然后便急切地等待午餐时间的到来。在这期间,我还得为工厂经理查尔斯·巴切勒先生解决各种难题,他是爱迪生的好友兼助手。在这里,我结识了几位美国朋友,他们都被我高超的台球技术折服。我向这些人介绍了我的发明,其中一位,机械部的领班坎宁安先生,提出要成立一家股份公司。这个提议在我看来可笑至极,除了知道这是一种美国人的

friend and assistant of Edison. Here I was thrown in contact with a few Americans who fairly fell in love with me because of my proficiency in—billiards. To these men I explained my invention and one of them, Mr. D. Cunningham, Foreman of the Mechanical Department, offered to form a stock company. The proposal seemed to me comical in the extreme. I did not have the faintest conception of what that meant except that it was an American way of doing things. Nothing came of it, however, and during the next few months I had to travel from one to another place in France and Germany to cure the ills of the power plants. On my return to Paris I submitted to one of the administrators of the Company, Mr. Rau, a plan for improving their dynamos and was given an opportunity. My success was complete and the delighted directors accorded me the privilege of developing automatic regulators which were much desired. Shortly after there was some trouble with the lighting plant which had been installed at the new railroad station in Strassburg, Alsace. The wiring was defective and on the occasion of the opening ceremonies a large part of a wall was blown out through a short-circuit right in the presence of old Emperor William I. The German Government refused to take the plant and the French Company was facing a serious loss. On account of my knowledge of the German language and past experience, I was entrusted with the difficult task of straightening out matters and early in 1883 I went to Strassburg on that mission.

做事方式外，我对此一点概念都没有。因此，这件事也就不了了之了。在接下来的几个月里，因为要处理发电站出现的问题，我不得不在法国和德国的各个城市间辗转。回到巴黎后，我向公司的一位高管劳先生提交了一份发电机改进方案，结果被采纳了。我圆满完成了这项任务，董事们非常满意，授权我研发自动调节器，而这正是我梦寐以求的。之后不久，在阿尔萨斯州斯特拉斯堡的新火车站安装的照明设备出现了一些问题。正值老皇帝威廉一世出席开幕式，线路出了问题，一堵墙的大部分因为短路被炸毁，德国政府因此拒绝接收这批设备，这家法国公司面临巨额损失。考虑到我会说德语以及过往的经验，我被委以重任。1883年初，我奉命前往斯特拉斯堡执行这一项艰巨的任务。

Some of the incidents in that city have left an indelible record on my memory. By a curious coincidence, a number of men who subsequently achieved fame, lived there about that time. In later life I used to say, "There were bacteria of greatness in that old town. Others caught the disease but I escaped!" The practical work, correspondence, and conferences with officials kept me preoccupied day and night, but, as soon as I was able to manage I undertook the construction of a simple motor in a mechanical shop opposite the railroad station, having brought with me from Paris some material for that purpose. The consummation of the experiment was, however, delayed until the summer of that year when I finally had the satisfaction of seeing rotation effected by alternating currents of different phase, and without sliding contacts or commutator, as I had conceived a year before. It was an exquisite pleasure but not to compare with the delirium of joy following the first revelation.

Among my new friends was the former Mayor of the city, Mr. Bauzin, whom I had already in a measure acquainted with this and other inventions of mine and whose support I endeavored to enlist. He was sincerely devoted to me and put my project before several wealthy persons but, to my mortification, found no response. He wanted to help me in every possible way and the approach of the first of July, 1919, happens to remind me of a form of "assistance" I received from that

在那座城市,有些事在我的记忆中留下了不可磨灭的痕迹。也许是巧合,我在那里的时候,一些后来成名的人也住在那里。在后来的生活中,我常说:"在那座古城里,有许多可怕的细菌。其他人受感染了,但我逃过了一劫!"每天我要处理日常事务,与官员通信、开会,疲于奔命。但是,一旦有空,我就会在火车站对面的一个机械车间里着手建造一台简单的电机,为此我还从巴黎带来了一些材料。然而,实验一直推迟到那年夏天才完成,我终于满意地看到我一年前设想的场景,在没有滑动接头或转向器的情况下,通过交替不同相位的电流产生了旋转磁场。这种快乐美妙至极,但仍无法与当初第一次得到启示后的狂喜相媲美。

在我的新朋友中,有该市的前市长鲍津先生,他知道我的这台装置和一些其他的发明,我也努力争取得到他的支持。他极力支持我,并把我的项目介绍给了几位富商,但令我沮丧的是,没有得到任何回应。他想尽一切办法帮助我,1919年7月1日的到来,恰好让我想起了我从这位可爱的先生那里得到的另一种"帮助",这种帮助虽然不是经济上的,但仍然让我铭记于

charming man, which was not financial but none the less appreciated. In 1870, when the Germans invaded the country, Mr. Bauzin had buried a good sized allotment of St. Estèphe of 1801 and he came to the conclusion that he knew no worthier person than myself to consume that precious beverage. This, I may say, is one of the unforgettable incidents to which I have referred. My friend urged me to return to Paris as soon as possible and seek support there. This I was anxious to do but my work and negotiations were protracted owing to all sorts of petty obstacles I encountered so that at times the situation seemed hopeless.

Just to give an idea of German thoroughness and "efficiency", I may mention here a rather funny experience. An incandescent lamp of 16 c.p. was to be placed in a hallway and upon selecting the proper location I ordered the monteur to run the wires. After working for a while he concluded that the engineer had to be consulted and this was done. The latter made several objections but ultimately agreed that the lamp should be placed two inches from the spot I had assigned, whereupon the work proceeded. Then the engineer became worried and told me that Inspector Averdeck should be notified. That important person called, investigated, debated, and decided that the lamp should be shifted back two inches, which was the place I had marked. It was not long, however, before Averdeck got cold feet himself and advised me that he had informed Ober-Inspector Hieronimus of the matter

心。1870年,当德国入侵法国时,鲍津先生埋下了一大批1801年的圣爱斯泰夫酒,他认定没有谁比我更配得上这款酒的了。这件事,可以说,算得上我前面提到的难忘回忆之一吧。我的朋友敦促我尽快返回巴黎,在那里寻求帮助。我也很着急,但由于各种各样的琐碎障碍,我的工作和谈判进展缓慢,很多时候,我都觉得陷入了死局。

为了让大家了解德国人的严谨和"效率",我可以讲一个相当搞笑的经历。走廊里要安一盏16瓦的白炽灯,在选好了合适的位置后,我喊来一名电工开始走线。倒腾了一会儿后,他认为这事需要征求工程师的意见。工程师来了后,提出了一些反对意见,但最终同意将灯放在离我指定的位置两英寸远的地方,于是工作继续进行,又过了一阵,工程师开始担心起来,告诉我应该通知质检员阿夫戴克。这位重要人物打来了电话,进行了调查和讨论,最后决定将灯向后移两英寸,就是我一开始所标记的地方。然而,没过多久,阿夫戴克也犹豫了起来,并告诉我他已经将此事上报质检督察希罗尼姆斯,我得等他的决定。几天后,质检督察才从其他紧急任务中抽出空来,终于来了,进行了长达两个小时的讨论,决定将灯再移两英寸。我原以为

and that I should await his decision. It was several days before the Ober-Inspector was able to free himself of other pressing duties but at last he arrived and a two-hour debate followed, when he decided to move the lamp two inches farther. My hopes that this was the final act were shattered when the Ober-Inspector returned and said to me: "Regierungsrath Funke is so particular that I would not dare to give an order for placing this lamp without his explicit approval." Accordingly arrangements for a visit from that great man were made. We started cleaning up and polishing early in the morning. Everybody brushed up, I put on my gloves and when Funke came with his retinue he was ceremoniously received. After two hours of deliberation he suddenly exclaimed: "I must be going," and pointing to a place on the ceiling, he ordered me to put the lamp there. It was the exact spot which I had originally chosen.

So it went day after day with variations, but I was determined to achieve at whatever cost and in the end my efforts were rewarded. By the spring of 1884 all the differences were adjusted, the plant formally accepted, and I returned to Paris with pleasing anticipations. One of the administrators had promised me a liberal compensation in case I succeeded, as well as a fair consideration of the improvements I had made in their dynamos and I hoped to realize a substantial sum. There were three administrators whom I shall designate as A, B and C for

这就是最后的结果,但他回来对我说:"芬克长官非常挑剔,没有他的明确批准,我不敢下达安装这盏灯的命令。"我崩溃了。于是,我们为这位重要领导的来访做了相应的安排。一大早我们就开始打扫卫生,每个人都精心梳洗打扮了一番,我还戴上了手套,当芬克带着他的随从到来时,受到了隆重的欢迎。经过两个小时的深思熟虑,他突然喊道:"我得走了。"然后指着天花板上的一个地方,命令我把灯安在那里,而那儿,正是我最初选择的地方。

就这样,每天都有这样那样的新状况,但我决心不惜一切代价也要实现目标,最终我的努力得到了回报。到了1884年春天,所有的分歧都得到了解决,设备被正式接收,我满怀憧憬回到了巴黎。公司的一位高管曾向我承诺,如果我成功了,将给予我丰厚的补偿,考虑到我在发电机上的改进,我觉得应该能得到一笔可观的收入。有三位高管,为了方便起见,我将他们称为甲、乙和丙吧。当我拜访甲时,他告诉我乙有发言权。

convenience. When I called on A he told me that B had the say. This gentleman thought that only C could decide and the latter was quite sure that A alone had the power to act. After several laps of this circulus viciosus, it dawned upon me that my reward was a castle in Spain. The utter failure of my attempts to raise capital for development was another disappointment and when Mr. Batchellor pressed me to go to America with a view of redesigning the Edison machines, I determined to try my fortunes in the Land of Golden Promise. But the chance was nearly missed. I liquefied my modest assets, secured accommodations and found myself at the railroad station as the train was pulling out. At that moment I discovered that my money and tickets were gone. What to do was the question. Hercules had plenty of time to deliberate but I had to decide while running alongside the train with opposite feelings surging in my brain like condenser oscillations. Resolve, helped by dexterity, won out in the nick of time and upon passing through the usual experiences, as trivial as unpleasant, I managed to embark for New York with the remnants of my belongings, some poems and articles I had written, and a package of calculations relating to solutions of an unsolvable integral and to my flying machine. During the voyage I sat most of the time at the stern of the ship watching for an opportunity to save somebody from a watery grave, without the slightest thought of danger. Later when I had absorbed some of the practical American

乙呢，认为只有丙可以决定，而丙非常肯定只有甲有权拍板。兜了几圈后，我恍然大悟，我的奖励就像海市蜃楼般可望而不可即。屋漏偏逢连夜雨，我为研发筹集资金的计划也彻底宣告失败，所以，当巴切勒先生希望我去美国为爱迪生公司重新设计机器时，我决定去这个"淘金圣地"碰碰运气。但这个机遇，我也差一点错失了。我变现了微薄的资产，检查了一遍出租屋，等赶到火车站时，火车就要开了。紧急关头，我却发现钱和车票都不见了。怎么办！赫拉克勒斯[①]（大力神）有足够的时间来思考，但我必须尽快抉择！我跟着火车奔跑，脑子里两种相反的念头激烈碰撞，此消彼长。关键时刻，去美国的决心最终还是胜出了。在经历了一系列琐碎、恼人的事情后，我带着我的剩余物品、之前写的诗和文章，还有一大捆关于一个无解积分和我设计的飞行器的计算结果，灵机一动，转而登上了前往纽约的轮船。在航行过程中，我大部分时间都坐在船尾，看有没有机会救不小心落水的人，丝毫没有考虑过自身安危。后来，当我吸收了一些美国人的实用主义精神后，再回想起此事，顿觉后怕，为自己的愚蠢感到无语。

---

① 古希腊神话中的一位半神，宙斯之子，天生力大无穷。

sense I shivered at the recollection and marvelled at my former folly.

I wish that I could put in words my first impressions of this country. In the Arabian Tales I read how genii transported people into a land of dreams to live through delightful adventures. My case was just the reverse. The genii had carried me from a world of dreams into one of realities. What I had left was beautiful, artistic and fascinating in every way; what I saw here was machined, rough and unattractive. A burly policeman was twirling his stick which looked to me as big as a log. I approached him politely with the request to direct me. "Six blocks down, then to the left," he said, with murder in his eyes. "Is this America?" I asked myself in painful surprise. "It is a century behind Europe in civilization." When I went abroad in 1889—five years having elapsed since my arrival here—I became convinced that it was more than one hundred years AHEAD of Europe and nothing has happened to this day to change my opinion.

The meeting with Edison was a memorable event in my life. I was amazed at this wonderful man who, without early advantages and scientific training, had accomplished so much. I had studied a dozen languages, delved in literature and art, and had spent my best years in libraries reading all sorts of stuff that fell into my hands, from Newton's "Principia" to the novels of Paul de Kock, and felt that most of my life

我希望能用语言表达出我对这个国家的第一印象。在阿拉伯故事中,精灵历经一系列轻松活泼的冒险,把人们带到了梦幻王国。我的情况正好相反,精灵把我从一个梦幻王国带到了现实世界。我离开的地方是美丽的、艺术的、迷人的,而我在这里看到的是机械的、粗糙的、无趣的。一个身材魁梧的警察正在转动他的警棍,在我看来,他的警棍像树干一样粗。我礼貌地走近他,向他问路,他说:"往南走六条街,然后左转。"他的眼神阴森可怕。"这是美国吗?"我痛苦而惊讶地问自己。"这里的文明落后欧洲一个世纪。"但当我1889年再出国时——我来美国已经过了五年——我开始相信,它不是落后,而是领先欧洲一百多年,直到现在我仍这么认为。

与爱迪生的会面是我生命中一个难忘的回忆。我由衷地佩服这位了不起的人物,既没有先天优势,也没有接受科学训练,却取得了如此大的成就。而我呢,学过十几种语言,钻研过文学和艺术,在最好的年纪里,一头扎进图书馆,从牛顿的《原

had been squandered. But it did not take long before I recognized that it was the best thing I could have done. Within a few weeks I had won Edison's confidence and it came about in this way.

The S.S. Oregon, the fastest passenger steamer at that time, had both of its lighting machines disabled and its sailing was delayed. As the superstructure had been built after their installation it was impossible to remove them from the hold. The predicament was a serious one and Edison was much annoyed. In the evening I took the necessary instruments with me and went aboard the vessel where I stayed for the night. The dynamos were in bad condition, having several short-circuits and breaks, but with the assistance of the crew I succeeded in putting them in good shape. At five o'clock in the morning, when passing along Fifth Avenue on my way to the shop, I met Edison with Batchellor and a few others as they were returning home to retire. "Here is our Parisian running around at night," he said. When I told him that I was coming from the Oregon and had repaired both machines, he looked at me in silence and walked away without another word. But when he had gone some distance I heard him remark: "Batchellor, this is a d—n good man," and from that time on I had full freedom in directing the work. For nearly a year my regular hours were from 10:30 A.M. until 5 o'clock the next morning without a day's exception. Edison said to me: "I have had many hard-working assistants but you take

第四章 特斯拉线圈和变压器的发现
IV. The Discovery of the Tesla Coil and Transformer

理》到保罗·德·科克的小说，碰到什么读什么，我觉得我的大部分光阴都虚度了。但没过多久，我就意识到这已是我能做的最好的事情了。不到几个星期，我就赢得了爱迪生的信任，事情是这样的：

俄勒冈号是当时最快的客轮，但两台发电机都坏了，无法航行。当初是发电机装好后，在上面建造的客舱，所以没办法将它们从船舱中移除。这种情况很麻烦，爱迪生非常恼火。那天晚上，我带着一些必备的仪器上了船，并在那忙活了一宿。发电机的状况很糟糕，有几处短路和断裂，但在船员的协助下，我把它们修好了。早上五点，我沿着第五大道去早餐店，遇到了爱迪生和巴切勒以及其他几个人，他们正准备回家休息。他说："这不是我们的巴黎人嘛，不知道去哪玩了一宿。"当我告诉他我刚从俄勒冈号下来并且已经修好了两台电机时，他默默地看着我，没有再说话就走了。但当他走了一段路后，我听到他说："巴切勒，这真是个大好人。"从那时起，我有了充分的自由来安排工作。在将近一年的时间里，我的正常工作时间是从上午10点半到第二天早上5点，没有一天例外。爱迪生对我说："我有过很多勤奋的助手，但你是最棒的。"在这期间，我设计了24种不同类型的标准机器，全部都是短芯，规格统一，取代了之前的老款。经理曾答应在完成这项任务后给我五万美

the cake." During this period I designed twenty-four different types of standard machines with short cores and of uniform pattern which replaced the old ones. The Manager had promised me fifty thousand dollars on the completion of this task but it turned out to be a practical joke. This gave me a painful shock and I resigned my position.

Immediately thereafter some people approached me with the proposal of forming an arc light company under my name, to which I agreed. Here finally was an opportunity to develop the motor, but when I broached the subject to my new associates they said: "No, we want the arc lamp. We don't care for this alternating current of yours." In 1886 my system of arc lighting was perfected and adopted for factory and municipal lighting, and I was free, but with no other possession than a beautifully engraved certificate of stock of hypothetical value. Then followed a period of struggle in the new medium for which I was not fitted, but the reward came in the end and in April, 1887, the Tesla Electric Company was organized, providing a laboratory and facilities. The motors I built there were exactly as I had imagined them. I made no attempt to improve the design, but merely reproduced the pictures as they appeared to my vision and the operation was always as I expected.

In the early part of 1888 an arrangement was made with the Westinghouse Company for the manufacture of the motors on a large

第四章 特斯拉线圈和变压器的发现
IV. The Discovery of the Tesla Coil and Transformer

元奖金，但结果却是一句玩笑话。这让我备受打击，意兴阑珊，于是我辞职了。

很快，就有人找到我，提议以我的名义成立一家弧光灯公司，我同意了。终于，我有了一个开发电机的机会，但当我向我的新伙伴提出这个设想时，他们说："不，我们要的是弧光灯。我们对你的交流电不感兴趣。"1886年，我的电弧照明系统在完善后，应用于工厂和市政照明。我也无事可干了，手头拥有的，不过是一张印刷精美但实际价值未知的股权证书。接下来的一段时间，我被迫在不适合自己的领域里挣扎，但最终，回报还是来了，1887年4月，特斯拉电气公司成立了，我有了一个实验室和一些相关的设备。我在那造出的电机与我当初设想的如出一辙，我没有试图改动，只是按照设想的样子还原了出来，运转效果也如我所料。

scale. But great difficulties had still to be overcome. My system was based on the use of low frequency currents and the Westinghouse experts had adopted 133 cycles with the object of securing advantages in the transformation. They did not want to depart from their standard forms of apparatus and my efforts had to be concentrated upon adapting the motor to these conditions. Another necessity was to produce a motor capable of running efficiently at this frequency on two wires which was not easy to accomplishment.

At the close of 1889, however, my services in Pittsburg being no longer essential, I returned to New York and resumed experimental work in a laboratory on Grand Street, where I began immediately the design of high frequency machines. The problems of construction in this unexplored field were novel and quite peculiar and I encountered many difficulties. I rejected the inductor type, fearing that it might not yield perfect sine waves which were so important to resonant action. Had it not been for this I could have saved myself a great deal of labor. Another discouraging feature of the high frequency alternator seemed to be the inconstancy of speed which threatened to impose serious limitations to its use. I had already noted in my demonstrations before the *American Institution of Electrical Engineers* that several times the tune was lost, necessitating readjustment, and did not yet foresee, what I discovered long afterwards, a means of operating a machine of this kind at a speed

1888 年初，我们与西屋公司达成了一项协议，准备大规模生产这种电机，但仍有一些棘手的问题需要解决。我的系统使用的是低频电流，而西屋公司的专家们为了确保变电优势，采用的是 133 周波。他们不想更改他们设备的标准形式，只能我来调整电机。另外，电机需要在两条线路上以这种频率高效运转，绝非易事。

到了 1889 年底，匹兹堡的工作已不再需要我，于是我回到了纽约，在格兰德街的一个实验室里继续工作，在那儿，我马不停蹄地开始了高频电机的设计。这个领域前人未曾涉足，我遇到了许多困难、很多新奇问题。我舍弃了感应电机方案，担心它可能无法产生完美的正弦波，而正弦波对谐振作用非常重要。要不是这个原因，我本可以节省大量的精力。高频交流发电机的另一个缺陷是速度不稳定，这可能会严重限制其应用。之前在美国电气工程师协会的演示中我已经注意到，电频有几次失灵，需要重新调整。我在发现此现象后过了很久，才想出一种方法，可以使这种机器保持恒定的速度运行，并使负载极限之间的变化极小且在可控范围内。

constant to such a degree as not to vary more than a small fraction of one revolution between the extremes of load.

From many other considerations it appeared desirable to invent a simpler device for the production of electric oscillations. In 1856 Lord Kelvin had exposed the theory of the condenser discharge, but no practical application of that important knowledge was made. I saw the possibilities and undertook the development of induction apparatus on this principle. My progress was so rapid as to enable me to exhibit at my lecture in 1891 a coil giving sparks of five inches. On that occasion I frankly told the engineers of a defect involved in the transformation by the new method, namely, the loss in the spark gap. Subsequent investigation showed that no matter what medium is employed, be it air, hydrogen, mercury vapor, oil or a stream of electrons, the efficiency is the same. It is a law very much like that governing the conversion of mechanical energy. We may drop a weight from a certain height vertically down or carry it to the lower level along any devious path, it is immaterial insofar as the amount of work is concerned. Fortunately however, this drawback is not fatal as by proper proportioning of the resonant circuits an efficiency of 85 per cent is attainable. Since my early announcement of the invention it has come into universal use and wrought a revolution in many departments. But a still greater future awaits it. When in 1900 I obtained powerful discharges of 100 feet and

第四章 特斯拉线圈和变压器的发现
IV. The Discovery of the Tesla Coil and Transformer

综合诸多其他因素，似乎有必要发明一种更简单的装置来产生电振荡。1856年，开尔文勋爵提出了电容器放电的理论，但这一重要理论并未得到实际应用。我觉得有可行性，于是着手研制基于这一原理的感应装置。我的进展十分神速，在1891年的演讲中，我已能展示一个可产生五英寸火花的线圈。不过那次我也坦率地告诉工程师们，新方法进行电能转换有一个缺陷，即火花间隙的损耗。随后的研究表明，不管采用何种介质，无论是空气、氢气、汞蒸气、油，还是电子流，效率都是一样的。这与机械能的转换定律非常相似。我们可以把一个重物从一定的高度垂直抛下，或沿着任何一条曲折的小路把它运到低处，不管消耗多少能量，机械能都是守恒的。然而，幸运的是，这个缺点并不致命，通过对谐振电路进行适当的配比，可以达到85%的效率。这项发明，自从我宣布以来，已得到广泛应用，并在许多领域引发了变革。但是，更好的前景还在未来。

flashed a current around the globe, I was reminded of the first tiny spark I observed in my Grand Street laboratory and was thrilled by sensations akin to those I felt when I discovered the rotating magnetic field.

1900年，我利用放电球制造出了100英尺长的强大放电，达成人造闪电效应，当时，我想起了在格兰德街实验室里观察到的第一个微小的火花，想起了我发现旋转磁场时的欣喜若狂，兴奋之情难以言表。

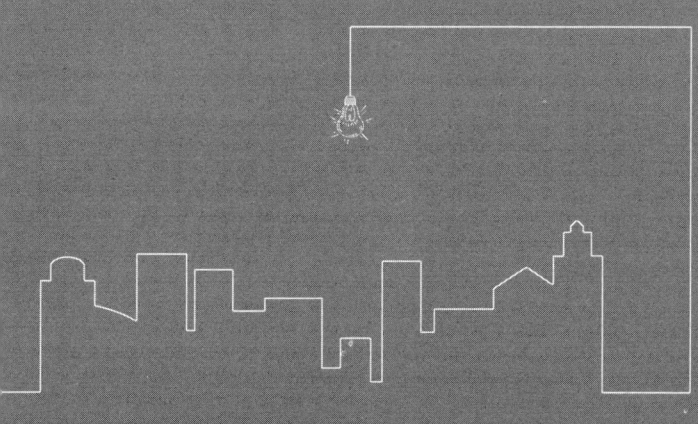

V. The Magnifying Transmitter

第五章 放大发射器

As I review the events of my past life I realize how subtle are the influences that shape our destinies. An incident of my youth may serve to illustrate. One winter's day I managed to climb a steep mountain, in company with other boys. The snow was quite deep and a warm southerly wind made it just suitable for our purpose. We amused ourselves by throwing balls which would roll down a certain distance, gathering more or less snow, and we tried to outdo one another in this exciting sport. Suddenly a ball was seen to go beyond the limit, swelling to enormous proportions until it became as big as a house and plunged thundering into the valley below with a force that made the ground tremble. I looked on spellbound, incapable of understanding what had happened. For weeks afterward the picture of the avalanche was before my eyes and I wondered how anything so small could grow to such an immense size. Ever since that time the magnification of feeble actions fascinated me, and when, years later, I took up the experimental study of mechanical and electrical resonance, I was keenly interested from the very start. Possibly, had it not been for that early powerful impression, I might not have followed up the little spark I obtained with my coil and never developed my best invention, the true history of which I'll tell here for the first time.

"Lionhunters" have often asked me which of my discoveries I prize most. This depends on the point of view. Not a few technical men,

第五章 放大发射器
V．The Magnifying Transmitter

回首过往种种，我意识到，决定我们命运的往往是那些微妙的瞬间。就拿我年少时的一件事来说吧，一个冬日，我和其他男孩子一道，去爬一座陡峭的山峰。积雪很深，温暖的南风十分舒适。我们玩起了扔雪球的游戏，雪球落地后，会继续滚一段距离，然后多少会裹上一些雪，我们很兴奋，都想超过对手，乐此不疲。突然，我看见一个雪球滚得很远，而且越滚越大，直到像一座房子那么大，然后冲下山谷，发出雷鸣般的声响，大地都为之颤抖。我看得目瞪口呆，完全不明白发生了什么。接下来的几个星期，雪崩的画面一直在我眼前浮现，我想知道，这么小的东西怎么能变得如此巨大。从那时起，我就痴迷于将微小力量变大，多年后，我开始了机械和谐振电路的实验，并一发不可收拾，沉醉其中。也许，如果不是儿时那次印象深刻的经历，我可能不会研究由我的线圈产生的那束小火花，我最杰出的发明也就不会问世。下面呢，我将首次跟大家说一说，关于这个发明的真实故事。

一些想巴结我的人经常问我，我最看重的发明是哪一个。这个嘛，要看从什么角度看。不少技术人员，在他们的专业领

very able in their special departments, but dominated by a pedantic spirit and nearsighted, have asserted that excepting the induction motor I have given to the world little of practical use. This is a grievous mistake. A new idea must not be judged by its immediate results. My alternating system of power transmission came at a psychological moment, as a long-sought answer to pressing industrial questions, and although considerable resistance had to be overcome and opposing interests reconciled, as usual, the commercial introduction could not be long delayed. Now, compare this situation with that confronting my turbine, for example. One should think that so simple and beautiful an invention, possessing many features of an ideal motor, should be adopted at once and, undoubtedly, it would under similar conditions. But the prospective effect of the rotating field was not to render worthless existing machinery; on the contrary, it was to give it additional value. The system lent itself to new enterprise as well as to improvement of the old. My turbine is an advance of a character entirely different. It is a radical departure in the sense that its success would mean the abandonment of the antiquated types of prime movers on which billions of dollars have been spent. Under such circumstances the progress must be slow and perhaps the greatest impediment is encountered in the prejudicial opinions created in the minds of experts by organized opposition.

第五章 放大发射器
V. The Magnifying Transmitter

域非常能干,但却迂腐且目光短浅。他们断言,除了感应电机外,我给这个世界带来的具有实际用途的东西很少。这是一个严重的误区,一个新的想法不能以其立竿见影的效果来判断,我的交流电传输系统,解决了长期以来工业生产迫在眉睫的问题,尽管与过往一样,必须克服相当大的阻力,调和对立的利益,但商业推广不可能会拖很久。现在,将这种情况与我的涡轮机当时所面临的情况进行比较,人们可能会认为,这样一个简单而美妙的发明,拥有理想电机的许多特性,应该立即投入使用,毫无疑问,在类似的条件下,是这样的。但是,旋转磁场的预期效果并不是让现有的机器变得毫无价值,相反,还会赋予它附加的价值。这个系统既有利于新的企业,也适合于对旧的企业进行改造。我的涡轮机是一种完全不同性质的进步,从某种意义上说,这是一种彻底的改变,因为它的成功意味着要放弃那些已经花费了数十亿美元的过时原动机。在这种情况下,进展必须放缓,也许最大的障碍是那些有偏见的专家的反对声。

Only the other day I had a disheartening experience when I met my friend and former assistant, Charles F. Scott, now professor of Electrical Engineering at Yale. I had not seen him for a long time and was glad to have an opportunity for a little chat at my office. Our conversation naturally enough drifted on my turbine and I became heated to a high degree. "Scott," I exclaimed, carried away by the vision of a glorious future, "my turbine will scrap all the heat-engines in the world." Scott stroked his chin and looked away thoughtfully, as though making a mental calculation. "That will make quite a pile of scrap," he said, and left without another word!

These and other inventions of mine, however, were nothing more than steps forward in certain directions. In evolving them I simply followed the inborn sense to improve the present devices without any special thought of our far more imperative necessities. The "Magnifying Transmitter" was the product of labors extending through years, having for their chief object the solution of problems which are infinitely more important to mankind than mere industrial development.

If my memory serves me right, it was in November, 1890, that I performed a laboratory experiment which was one of the most extraordinary and spectacular ever recorded in the ANNALS OF SCIENCE. In investigating the behaviour of high frequency currents

第五章 放大发射器
V. The Magnifying Transmitter

就在前几天，我遇到了一件令人沮丧的事，我见到了我的朋友兼前助手查尔斯·斯科特，他现在是耶鲁大学的电气工程学教授。我已经很久没有见过他了，很高兴能有机会在我的办公室里坐下来聊一聊。我们的谈话自然而然地转向了我的涡轮机，我变得非常激动。"斯科特，"我沉醉在对美好未来的憧憬中感叹道，"我的涡轮机将淘汰世界上所有的热能发动机。"斯科特摸了摸下巴，若有所思地望向别处，似乎在做着什么打算。"那将会多出好大一堆废铁啊！"他说道，然后一言不发就离开了！

然而，我的这些发明，还有其他的发明，只不过是在某些方面向前迈进了几步。在做这些发明时，我只是遵循与生俱来的感觉来改进现有的设备，而没有特别考虑我们更迫切的需求。"放大发射器"是我潜心研究多年的成果，其主要目的是解决对人类来说无比重要的问题，而不单单是工业发展。

如果我没记错的话，那是在1890年的11月，我在实验室做了一个实验，这是《科学年鉴》中记载的有史以来最特别、最壮观的一次实验。之前在研究高频电流时，我惊喜地发现，在一定空间里可以产生足够强度的电场来点亮无电极真空管。因

I had satisfied myself that an electric field of sufficient intensity could be produced in a room to light up electrodeless vacuum tubes. Accordingly, a transformer was built to test the theory and the first trial proved a marvelous success. It is difficult to appreciate what those strange phenomena meant at that time. We crave for new sensations but soon become indifferent to them. The wonders of yesterday are today common occurrences. When my tubes were first publicly exhibited they were viewed with amazement impossible to describe. From all parts of the world I received urgent invitations and numerous honors and other flattering inducements were offered to me, which I declined.

But in 1892 the demands became irresistible and I went to London where I delivered a lecture before the *Institution of Electrical Engineers*. It had been my intention to leave immediately for Paris in compliance with a similar obligation, but Sir James Dewar insisted on my appearing before the Royal Institution. I was a man of firm resolve but succumbed easily to the forceful arguments of the great Scotsman. He pushed me into a chair and poured out half a glass of a wonderful brown fluid which sparkled in all sorts of iridescent colors and tasted like nectar. "Now," said he, "you are sitting in Faraday's chair and you are enjoying whiskey he used to drink." In both aspects it was an enviable experience. The next evening I gave a demonstration before that Institution, at the termination of which Lord Rayleigh addressed

第五章 放大发射器
Ⅴ．The Magnifying Transmitter

此，我建了一台变压器来测试这一理论，第一次实验就取得了意想不到的成功。在当时，人们很难理解这些奇怪的现象意味着什么。我们渴望新刺激，但很快又变得熟视无睹。昨日的奇迹，在今天变成司空见惯的事。当我的真空管首次公开展示时，人们都投以无法形容的惊奇眼光，来自世界各地的邀请，伴随着无数的荣誉和诱惑接连不断，我都拒绝了。

但在1892年，邀约变得无法抗拒，我前往伦敦，在电气工程师协会做了一次演讲。我本打算立即前往巴黎参加类似的讲座，但詹姆斯·杜瓦爵士坚持要我访问皇家学会。我本是一个意志坚定的人，但很快就折服于他强有力的说辞，这个苏格兰人太厉害了。他把我推到一张椅子上，倒出半杯奇妙的棕色液体，闪烁着各种颜色，尝起来像花蜜。"现在，"他说道，"你正坐在法拉第的椅子上，享用着他常喝的威士忌。"无论从哪方面来看，这都是一次令人羡慕的经历。第二天晚上，我在皇家学会做了一次演讲，结束时，瑞利勋爵向观众发表了讲话，观众的反应和他的褒奖让我备受鼓舞，决定心无旁骛，致力于这些尝试。于是，我逃离了伦敦，又逃离了巴黎，逃离了对我的所有追捧，回到了家乡，在那里我经历了最痛苦的折磨和疾病。恢

the audience and his generous words gave me the first start in these endeavors. I fled from London and later from Paris to escape favors showered upon me, and journeyed to my home where I passed through a most painful ordeal and illness. Upon regaining my health I began to formulate plans for the resumption of work in America. Up to that time I never realized that I possessed any particular gift of discovery but Lord Rayleigh, whom I always considered as an ideal man of science, had said so and if that was the case I felt that I should concentrate on some big idea.

One day, as I was roaming in the mountains, I sought shelter from an approaching storm. The sky became overhung with heavy clouds but somehow the rain was delayed until, all of a sudden, there was a lightning flash and a few moments after a deluge. This observation set me thinking. It was manifest that the two phenomena were closely related, as cause and effect, and a little reflection led me to the conclusion that the electrical energy involved in the precipitation of the water was inconsiderable, the function of lightning being much like that of a sensitive trigger.

Here was a stupendous possibility of achievement. If we could produce electric effects of the required quality, this whole planet and the conditions of existence on it could be transformed. The sun raises

第五章 放大发射器
V. The Magnifying Transmitter

复健康后,我开始制订在美国继续工作的计划。在此之前,我从未意识到我拥有任何特殊的发明天赋,但我一直视为理想科学家的瑞利勋爵却觉得我有,如果真是这样的话,我觉得我应该把精力集中在一些震惊世界的想法上。

有一天,当我在山间漫步时,为了躲避即将到来的暴风雨,我找了一处避雨。天空中笼罩着厚厚的云层,但不知何故,雨迟迟未下,直到突然间,划过一道闪电,片刻过后,一场暴雨倾盆而下。这一景象不禁让我开始思考,很明显,这两种现象是密切相关的,存在着某种因果关系,稍加思索,我得出了结论,降水过程中的电能是无法估量的,而闪电的作用就像一个灵敏触发器。

念及此,我觉得有可能取得一项惊人的成就。如果我们能够产生所需的电效应,整个地球和人类的生存环境就可能被彻底改变。太阳使海水蒸发,风把水蒸气吹到遥远的地方,保持

the water of the oceans and winds drive it to distant regions where it remains in a state of most delicate balance. If it were in our power to upset it when and wherever desired, this mighty life-sustaining stream could be at will controlled. We could irrigate arid deserts, create lakes and rivers and provide motive power in unlimited amounts. This would be the most efficient way of harnessing the sun to the uses of man. The consummation depended on our ability to develop electric forces of the order of those in nature. It seemed a hopeless undertaking, but I made up my mind to try it and immediately on my return to the United States, in the Summer of 1892, work was begun which was to me all the more attractive, because a means of the same kind was necessary for the successful transmission of energy without wires.

The first gratifying result was obtained in the spring of the succeeding year when I reached tensions of about 1,000,000 volts with my conical coil. That was not much in the light of the present art, but it was then considered a feat. Steady progress was made until the destruction of my laboratory by fire in 1895, as may be judged from an article by T. C. Martin which appeared in the April number of the CENTURY MAGAZINE. This calamity set me back in many ways and most of that year had to be devoted to planning and reconstruction. However, as soon as circumstances permitted, I returned to the task.

第五章 放大发射器
Ⅴ. The Magnifying Transmitter

着最微妙的平衡状态。如果我们有能力在任何时间和地点对这种平衡进行干预，就可以随意掌控这个强大的生命维持系统。我们可以灌溉干旱的沙漠、创造湖泊和河流，以及提供无穷无尽的动力。这将是利用太阳为人类服务的最有效方式。这一成果取决于我们是否有能力开发出与自然界一样充沛的电力。这项任务看似天方夜谭，但我下定决心要试一试。于是，我立刻回到美国，并于1892年夏天开始了这项工作，这对我来说具有空前的吸引力，因为要想成功实现无线传输能量，这是必备条件。

第一个令人满意的结果是在来年春天获得的，当时我的锥形线圈达到了大约100万伏特的电压。从如今的技术角度来看，这并不算什么，但在当时是一项壮举。我们的工作一直在稳步推进，直到1895年我的实验室被一场大火吞噬殆尽，这件事，可以在当年《世纪杂志》4月刊登的一篇T.C.马丁的文章中得到证实。这场灾难让我的许多工作付之一炬，那一年大部分时间都不得不用于规划和重建。但是，一旦情况允许，我又重新投入了工作。

Although I knew that higher electro-motive forces were attainable with apparatus of larger dimensions, I had an instinctive perception that the object could be accomplished by the proper design of a comparatively small and compact transformer. In carrying on tests with a secondary in the form of a flat spiral, as illustrated in my patents, the absence of streamers surprised me, and it was not long before I discovered that this was due to the position of the turns and their mutual action. Profiting from this observation I resorted to the use of a high tension conductor with turns of considerable diameter sufficiently separated to keep down the distributed capacity, while at the same time preventing undue accumulation of the charge at any point. The application of this principle enabled me to produce pressures of 4,000,000 volts, which was about the limit obtainable in my new laboratory at Houston Street, as the discharges extended through a distance of 16 feet. A photograph of this transmitter was published in the ELECTRICAL REVIEW of November, 1898.

In order to advance further along this line I had to go into the open, and in the spring of 1899, having completed preparations for the erection of a wireless plant, I went to Colorado where I remained for more than one year. Here I introduced other improvements and refinements which made it possible to generate currents of any tension that may be desired. Those who are interested will find some

第五章 放大发射器
V. The Magnifying Transmitter

虽然我知道用更大的设备可以获得更高的电动势,但我本能地感觉,如果设计得当,一个小且紧凑的变压器就可以实现这一目标。正如我的专利所示,在对一个扁平螺旋式的次级线圈进行测试时,并没有电弧出现,这让我感到很惊讶,不久我就发现,这是由线圈匝的位置以及匝与匝之间的相互作用造成的。我从这一观察中获益,于是改用了一种较大直径的高压导体,保证足够的匝间距,以降低电容分布,同时防止电荷在任何一点过度堆积。遵循这一原理,我能产生 400 万伏特的电压,这差不多是我在休斯敦街的新实验室中所能达到的极限了,放电可以延伸到 16 英尺的距离。这台发射器的照片刊登在 1898 年 11 月的《电气评论》上。

为了在这条道路上更进一步,我必须到户外去实验,于是开始谋划建造一个无线电站,并在筹备工作结束后,于 1899 年春天前往科罗拉多州,在那里待了一年多。其间,我进一步改进了发射器,使之有可能产生任意所需强度的电流。如果有人想了解我在那里所做实验的相关信息,可以查阅 1900 年 6 月我在《世纪杂志》上发表的文章《增加人类能源的问题》,我在之

information in regard to the experiments I conducted there in my article, "The Problem of Increasing Human Energy" in the CENTURY MAGAZINE of June, 1900, to which I have referred on a previous occasion.

I have been asked by the ELECTRICAL EXPERIMENTER to be quite explicit on this subject so that my young friends among the readers of the magazine will clearly understand the construction and operation of my "Magnifying Transmitter" and the purposes for which it is intended. Well, then, in the first place, it is a resonant transformer with a secondary in which the parts, charged to a high potential, are of considerable area and arranged in space along ideal enveloping surfaces of very large radii of curvature, and at proper distances from one another thereby insuring a small electric surface density everywhere so that no leak can occur even if the conductor is bare. It is suitable for any frequency, from a few to many thousands of cycles per second, and can be used in the production of currents of tremendous volume and moderate pressure, or of smaller amperage and immense electromotive force. The maximum electric tension is merely dependent on the curvature of the surfaces on which the charged elements are situated and the area of the latter.

Judging from my past experience, as much as 100,000,000 volts

第五章 放大发射器
V．The Magnifying Transmitter

前也提到过这篇文章。

　　《电气实验者》希望我能对这项发明说得更详细些，这样他们的年轻读者朋友可以清楚地了解我的"放大发射器"的结构、操作以及用途。好吧，首先，它是一个带有次级线圈的谐振变压器，其中被充电到高电压的部件具有相当大的面积，沿着曲率半径非常大的理想包络面排列，并且彼此之间有适当的距离，从而确保各处的表面电荷密度都很小，这样，即使导体裸露，也不会漏电。适用于任何频率，从每秒几转到上万转，用于产生电流量极大而电压较小，或安培较小而电动势极大的电流。电压的最大值完全取决于充电元件所在的曲面曲率及表面积。

　　根据我以往的经验，产生高达上亿伏特的电压是完全可行

are perfectly practicable. On the other hand currents of many thousands of amperes may be obtained in the antenna. A plant of but very moderate dimensions is required for such performances. Theoretically, a terminal of less than 90 feet in diameter is sufficient to develop an electromotive force of that magnitude while for antenna currents of from 2,000–4,000 amperes at the usual frequencies it need not be larger than 30 feet in diameter.

In a more restricted meaning this wireless transmitter is one in which the Hertz-wave radiation is an entirely negligible quantity as compared with the whole energy, under which condition the damping factor is extremely small and an enormous charge is stored in the elevated capacity. Such a circuit may then be excited with impulses of any kind, even of low frequency and it will yield sinusoidal and continuous oscillations like those of an alternator.

Taken in the narrowest significance of the term, however, it is a resonant transformer which, besides possessing these qualities, is accurately proportioned to fit the globe and its electrical constants and properties, by virtue of which design it becomes highly efficient and effective in the wireless transmission of energy. Distance is then absolutely eliminated, there being no diminution in the intensity of the transmitted impulses. It is even possible to make the actions increase

的。另外，通过天线亦可获得数千安培的电流。一台尺寸适中的设备就可以实现这一目标。从理论上讲，一台直径不到90英尺的终端就足以产生如此大的电动势，而在一般频率下，使用天线获得2000—4000安培的电流，其直径不须超过30英尺。

从更严格的意义来说，这种无线发射器的赫兹波辐射与整个能量相比完全可以忽略不计，在这种情况下，阻尼系数极小，大量的电荷被存储在扩充的电容器中。这样的电路可以被任何类型的脉冲激发，甚至是低频率脉冲，并会产生像交流发电机那样的正弦连续振荡。

然而，退一万步来说，它是一个谐振变压器，除了拥有这些特性，还可以通过设置精确比例来匹配地球的电常数及其特性，凭借这种设计，在无线传输能量方面变得十分高效。如此一来，距离已完全不是问题，传输脉冲的强度丝毫不会减弱。甚至有可能根据精确的数学法则，随着距离的增加，强度不减反增。

with the distance from the plant according to an exact mathematical law.

This invention was one of a number comprised in my "World-System" of wireless transmission which I undertook to commercialize on my return to New York in 1900. As to the immediate purposes of my enterprise, they were clearly outlined in a technical statement of that period from which I quote:

"The 'World-System' has resulted from a combination of several original discoveries made by the inventor in the course of long continued research and experimentation. It makes possible not only the instantaneous and precise wireless transmission of any kind of signals, messages or characters, to all parts of the world, but also the interconnection of the existing telegraph, telephone, and other signal stations without any change in their present equipment. By its means, for instance, a telephone subscriber here may call up and talk to any other subscriber on the globe. An inexpensive receiver, not bigger than a watch, will enable him to listen anywhere, on land or sea, to a speech delivered or music played in some other place, however distant. These examples are cited merely to give an idea of the possibilities of this great scientific advance, which annihilates distance and makes

第五章 放大发射器
V. The Magnifying Transmitter

这项发明是构成我无线传输"世界系统"其中的一项，1900年回到纽约后，我开始着手它的商业化运作。至于公司的发展目标，在当时的技术声明中有明确的概述，现摘录如下：

"世界系统"是由发明者在长期的研究和实验过程中所取得的几个原始发现结合而成的。它不仅使各种信号、信息或文字即时精确地无线传输到世界各地，而且还使现有的电报、电话和其他信号站间的相互连接成为可能，无须对现有设备进行任何改变。例如，通过这种方式，一个电话用户可以打电话给地球上的任何用户并与之交谈。一个手表大小的廉价接收器，可以让他在陆地或海洋上的任何地方，收听全球各地的演讲或音乐。列举这些例子只是粗略描绘一下这一伟大科学进步的应用前景，它消除了距离的限制，仅凭一根电线，就可以使地球这个完美的自然导体在人类聪明才智所能想到的各个领域发挥作用。这个系统的一个深远影响是，对于任何设备，只要受一根或多根电线操控（操控距离明显受限），我们都可以不借助任何人造导体，在一个不受限制的距离（只要不超出地球的物理空间）激活它，并使它以同样的功能和精确度运行。因此，这种

that perfect natural conductor, the Earth, available for all the innumerable purposes which human ingenuity has found for a line-wire. One far-reaching result of this is that any device capable of being operated through one or more wires (at a distance obviously restricted) can likewise be actuated, without artificial conductors and with the same facility and accuracy, at distances to which there are no limits other than those imposed by the physical dimensions of the globe. Thus, not only will entirely new fields for commercial exploitation be opened up by this ideal method of transmission but the old ones vastly extended.

"The 'World-System' is based on the application of the following important inventions and discoveries:

"1. The 'Tesla Transformer'. This apparatus is in the production of electrical vibrations as revolutionary as gunpowder was in warfare. Currents many times stronger than any ever generated in the usual ways, and sparks over one hundred feet long, have been produced by the inventor with an instrument of this kind.

"2. The 'Magnifying Transmitter'. This is Tesla's best invention, a peculiar transformer specially adapted to excite the Earth, which is in the transmission of electrical energy what

第五章 放大发射器
V. The Magnifying Transmitter

理想的传输方式不仅为商业开辟了全新的领域,也为现有领域带来了广阔的拓展空间。

"世界系统"主要是基于以下重要发明和发现的应用:

1. 特斯拉变压器

这个装置给电磁振动领域带来了革命性的作用,不亚于火药之于战争。发明者使用这种仪器输出的电流,比通过任何一种传统方式输出的电流要强许多倍,并且能产生一百多英尺的火花。

2. 放大发射器

这是特斯拉最伟大的发明,它是一个特殊变压器,经过精确调试可以激活地球磁场,在电能传输方面的作用堪比望远镜

the telescope is in astronomical observation. By the use of this marvelous device he has already set up electrical movements of greater intensity than those of lightning and passed a current, sufficient to light more than two hundred incandescent lamps, around the globe.

"3. The 'Tesla Wireless System'. This system comprises a number of improvements and is the only means known for transmitting economically electrical energy to a distance without wires. Careful tests and measurements in connection with an experimental station of great activity, erected by the inventor in Colorado, have demonstrated that power in any desired amount can be conveyed, clear across the globe if necessary, with a loss not exceeding a few per cent.

"4. The 'Art of Individualization'. This invention of Tesla's is to primitive 'tuning' what refined language is to unarticulated expression. It makes possible the transmission of signals or messages absolutely secret and exclusive both in the active and passive aspect, that is, non-interfering as well as non-interferable. Each signal is like an individual of unmistakable identity and there is virtually no limit to the number of stations or instruments which can be simultaneously operated without the slightest mutual disturbance.

之于天文观测。使用这个神奇装置，发明者已经实现了比闪电强度更大的电力效应，输送的电流，足以点亮全球 200 多盏白炽灯。

3. 特斯拉无线系统

这个系统包含多项先进技术，是目前已知的唯一可以低成本、远距离无线传输电能的系统。发明者在科罗拉多州建立了一个实验站，进行了多次精心测试和计算，结果表明，不管多大功率的电力都可以在全球范围内传输，且损耗不超过几个百分点。

4. 个性化艺术

特斯拉的这项发明对于原始的"调谐"来说，好比精练的语言之于含糊的表达。这项技术，实现了信号或信息发送和接收的绝对私密和排他性，也就是说，既不干扰别人，也不受别人干扰。每一个信号就像一个拥有明确身份的个体，不管有多少个信号站或多少条线路同时工作，都不会有丝毫干扰。

"5. The 'Terrestrial Stationary Waves'. This wonderful discovery, popularly explained, means that the Earth is responsive to electrical vibrations of definite pitch just as a tuning fork to certain waves of sound. These particular electrical vibrations, capable of powerfully exciting the globe, lend themselves to innumerable uses of great importance commercially and in many other respects.

"The first 'World-System' power plant can be put in operation in nine months. With this power plant it will be practicable to attain electrical activities up to ten million horsepower and it is designed to serve for as many technical achievements as are possible without due expense. Among these the following may be mentioned:

"(1) The inter-connection of the existing telegraph exchanges or offices all over the world;

"(2) The establishment of a secret and non-interferable government telegraph service;

"(3) The inter-connection of all the present telephone exchanges or offices on the globe;

5. 陆地驻波

这一绝妙的发明，通俗地说，就是指地球对特定波长的电磁振动有反应，好比音叉之于特定音波一样。这些特殊的电磁振动，能够有效激活地球磁场，在商业和其他诸多领域大有可为。

第一座"世界系统"发电站预计将在 9 个月内投入使用。有了这个发电站，就可以实现高达 1000 万马力的功率，从而以较低的成本用于诸多技术革新领域。下面仅列举几项：

（1）世界各地现有的电报交换机或交换站之间的相互连接；

（2）私密的、不受干扰的政府电报服务系统的建立；

（3）全球现有的电话交换机或电话局之间的相互连接；

"(4) The universal distribution of general news, by telegraph or telephone, in connection with the press;

"(5) The establishment of such a 'World-System' of intelligence transmission for exclusive private use;

"(6) The inter-connection and operation of all stock tickers of the world;

"(7) The establishment of a 'World-System' of musical distribution, etc.;

"(8) The universal registration of time by cheap clocks indicating the hour with astronomical precision and requiring no attention whatever;

"(9) The world transmission of typed or handwritten characters, letters, checks, etc.;

"(10) The establishment of a universal marine service enabling the navigators of all ships to steer perfectly without compass, to determine the exact location, hour and speed, to prevent collisions and disasters, etc.;

"(11) The inauguration of a system of world-printing on land

第五章 放大发射器
Ⅴ. The Magnifying Transmitter

（4）通过电报或电话与新闻界连接，实现一般性新闻的全球传播；

（5）仅供私人使用的情报传输"世界系统"的建立；

（6）全球各地股票交易系统的相互连接和运作；

（7）音乐发行"世界系统"的建立；

（8）通过便宜的时钟实现计时，精度却堪比天文级，且无须维护；

（9）打印或手写的字符、信件、支票等的全球传送；

（10）全球航海服务系统的建立，有此系统，所有船只不使用罗盘即可完美航行，精准确定位置、时间和速度，防止碰撞和其他事故等；

（11）陆海一体的全球地貌测绘系统的启用；

and sea;

"(12) The world reproduction of photographic pictures and all kinds of drawings or records."

I also proposed to make demonstrations in the wireless transmission of power on a small scale but sufficient to carry conviction. Besides these I referred to other and incomparably more important applications of my discoveries which will be disclosed at some future date.

A plant was built on Long Island with a tower 187 feet high, having a spherical terminal about 68 feet in diameter. These dimensions were adequate for the transmission of virtually any amount of energy. Originally only from 200 to 300 K.W. were provided but I intended to employ later several thousand horsepower. The transmitter was to emit a wave complex of special characteristics and I had devised a unique method of telephonic control of any amount of energy.

The tower was destroyed two years ago but my projects are being developed and another one, improved in some features, will be constructed. On this occasion I would contradict the widely circulated report that the structure was demolished by the Government which owing to war conditions, might have created prejudice in the minds

第五章 放大发射器
V. The Magnifying Transmitter

（12）摄影图片、各种绘画或记录在全球范围内的复制。

我还提议演示一下电力的无线传输，传输的电力可以不大，但要足以让人信服。除此之外，我的发明还有一些其他极其重要的应用，在将来我会公之于众。

我们在长岛建了一个发电站，高 187 英尺，顶部有一个直径约 68 英尺的球形终端发射塔。这个尺寸足以传输任何数值的能量。最初我们只有 200 至 300 千瓦的功率，但后来我打算增加到几千千瓦。该发射器可以发射特殊的复合波，我已设计出一种独特的方法，可以用电话控制任何数值的能量。

发射塔在两年前被毁，但我的研究并未中断，另一座塔即将建成，并在某些方面有了改进。在此，我想反驳一条广为人知的传闻，说出于备战考虑，这个塔是被美国政府拆除的，这可能会使一些人产生偏见，而他们不知道的是，30 年前授予我

of those who may not know that the papers, which thirty years ago conferred upon me the honor of American citizenship, are always kept in a safe, while my orders, diplomas, degrees, gold medals and other distinctions are packed away in old trunks. If this report had a foundation I would have been refunded a large sum of money which I expended in the construction of the tower. On the contrary it was in the interest of the Government to preserve it, particularly as it would have made possible—to mention just one valuable result—the location of a submarine in any part of the world. My plant, services, and all my improvements have always been at the disposal of the officials and ever since the outbreak of the European conflict I have been working at a sacrifice on several inventions of mine relating to aerial navigation, ship propulsion and wireless transmission which are of the greatest importance to the country. Those who are well informed know that my ideas have revolutionized the industries of the United States and I am not aware that there lives an inventor who has been, in this respect, as fortunate as myself especially as regards the use of his improvements in the war. I have refrained from publicly expressing myself on this subject before as it seemed improper to dwell on personal matters while all the world was in dire trouble.

I would add further, in view of various rumors which have reached me, that Mr. J. Pierpont Morgan did not interest himself with me in a

第五章 放大发射器
V . The Magnifying Transmitter

美国公民身份的文件一直保存在保险柜里,颁发给我的勋章、证书、学位、金牌和其他荣誉证明也都锁在旧箱子里。如果这个报告有依据的话,我本可以得到一大笔赔偿金,以补偿我建造发射塔所花费的资金。相反,保留发射塔才符合政府利益,仅举一例来说明它的价值,它可以定位世界上任何地方的潜艇。我的工厂、研究和我所有的先进技术一直由政府支配,自从欧洲冲突爆发以来,我一直不计报酬,致力于航空导航、船舶动力和无线传输方面的研究,这些对美国来说都是至关重要的。那些消息灵通的人士知道,我的发明给美国工业带来了翻天覆地的变化,我不知道还有哪位发明家在这方面有我这样幸运,特别是我的发明成果在战争中的应用。之前我一直避免在这个问题上公开发表自己的观点,因为当全世界都深陷泥沼的时候,强调个人问题似乎不太恰当。

鉴于我听到的各种谣言,我还要进一步补充下,约翰·皮尔庞特·摩根先生对我的研究的兴趣并非出自商业角度,而是

business way but in the same large spirit in which he has assisted many other pioneers. He carried out his generous promise to the letter and it would have been most unreasonable to expect from him anything more. He had the highest regard for my attainments and gave me every evidence of his complete faith in my ability to ultimately achieve what I had set out to do. I am unwilling to accord to some smallminded and jealous individuals the satisfaction of having thwarted my efforts. These men are to me nothing more than microbes of a nasty disease. My project was retarded by laws of nature. The world was not prepared for it. It was too far ahead of time. But the same laws will prevail in the end and make it a triumphal success.

第五章 放大发射器
Ⅴ．The Magnifying Transmitter

源自一种崇高的精神，之前他也因此而帮助过许多其他的先驱者。他兑现了他所有的慷慨承诺，如果还对他有更多的期望，那是非常不近人情的。他对我的成就给予了至高的评价，并完全相信我有能力最终实现我的目标。我不愿意让一些心胸狭窄、嫉贤妒能的人因我的努力遭到挫败而获得满足感。对我来说，这些人只不过是一群令人生厌的宵小之辈。我的项目是受阻于自然法则，当今世界并没有为此做好准备，它太超前了。但同样的法则最终将占领上风，我的项目也终将大获全胜。

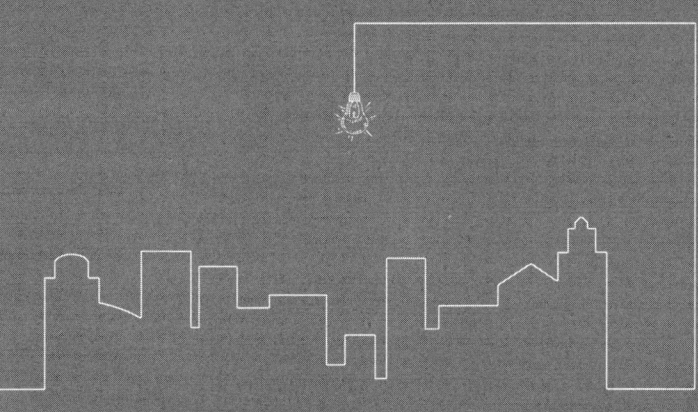

VI. The Art of Telautomatics
第六章 遥控力学的艺术

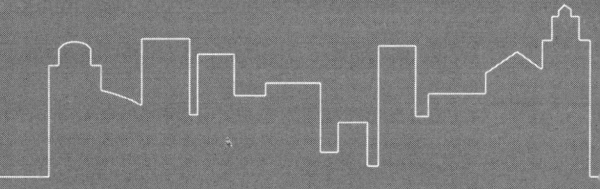

No subject to which I have ever devoted myself has called for such concentration of mind and strained to so dangerous a degree the finest fibers of my brain as the system of which the Magnifying Transmitter is the foundation. I put all the intensity and vigor of youth in the development of the rotating field discoveries, but those early labors were of a different character. Although strenuous in the extreme, they did not involve that keen and exhausting discernment which had to be exercised in attacking the many puzzling problems of the wireless. Despite my rare physical endurance at that period the abused nerves finally rebelled and I suffered a complete collapse, just as the consummation of the long and difficult task was almost in sight.

Without doubt I would have paid a greater penalty later, and very likely my career would have been prematurely terminated, had not providence equipped me with a safety device, which has seemed to improve with advancing years and unfailingly comes into play when my forces are at an end. So long as it operates I am safe from danger, due to overwork, which threatens other inventors and, incidentally, I need no vacations which are indispensable to most people. When I am all but used up I simply do as the darkies, who "naturally fall asleep while white folks worry". To venture a theory out of my sphere, the body probably accumulates little by little a definite quantity of some toxic agent and I sink into a nearly lethargic state which lasts half an

第六章 遥控力学的艺术
VI. The Art of Telautomatics

　　我曾潜心于诸多发明，但没有哪一件比得上这个基于放大发射器的系统耗费我如此多的精力，让我绞尽脑汁，几近崩溃。在旋转磁场的发现和研究上，我倾注了一个年轻人的所有热情和精力。与之相比，我早年的那些工作根本不值一提。虽然之前也极为辛苦，但并不需要这般敏锐且磨人的洞察力去解决无线传输的许多令人困惑的问题。那段时间里，尽管我的忍耐力异于常人，但超负荷工作的神经最终还是不堪重负，就在这项漫长而艰巨的任务即将完成之际，我彻底崩溃了。

　　毫无疑问，要不是老天爷给我配备了一个安全装置，我以后会付出更大的代价，我的发明生涯也很可能会早早终结。这个装置似乎会随着年龄的增长不断改进，在我精疲力竭时，就会出面接管。只要它还在工作，我就不会像其他发明家一样，因为过劳而面临危险。顺便说一句，我不需要休假，这对大多数人来说可能是不可或缺的。我在力竭之时，就会像黑人一样"自然地睡着，而不是跟大多数白人一样坐卧不宁"。在这里，我大胆提一个不在我研究领域的理论，我的身体可能慢慢积累了一定数量的某种"毒素"，能让我陷入一种近乎昏睡的状态，每次持续半个小时。醒来后，我有一种感觉，好像昏睡之前发生的事已经过了很久，如果我试图继续刚才中断的思路，就会

hour to the minute. Upon awakening I have the sensation as though the events immediately preceding had occurred very long ago, and if I attempt to continue the interrupted train of thought I feel a veritable mental nausea. Involuntarily I then turn to other work and am surprised at the freshness of the mind and ease with which I overcome obstacles that had baffled me before. After weeks or months my passion for the temporarily abandoned invention returns and I invariably find answers to all the vexing questions with scarcely any effort.

In this connection I will tell of an extraordinary experience which may be of interest to students of psychology. I had produced a striking phenomenon with my grounded transmitter and was endeavoring to ascertain its true significance in relation to the currents propagated through the earth. It seemed a hopeless undertaking, and for more than a year I worked unremittingly, but in vain. This profound study so entirely absorbed me that I became forgetful of everything else, even of my undermined health. At last, as I was at the point of breaking down, nature applied the preservative inducing lethal sleep. Regaining my senses I realized with consternation that I was unable to visualize scenes from my life except those of infancy, the very first ones that had entered my consciousness. Curiously enough, these appeared before my vision with startling distinctness and afforded me welcome relief. Night after night, when retiring, I would think of them and more and more

第六章 遥控力学的艺术
VI. The Art of Telautomatics

有一种强烈的恶心感。迫于无奈,我只好去做点别的事,然后惊讶地发现,整个人变得神清气爽,很轻松就解决了以前困扰我的难题。就这样,几周或几个月后,我对暂时搁置的发明的热情又回来了,无一例外,我几乎不费吹灰之力就找到了所有烦人问题的答案。

在这方面,我想讲述一段不同寻常的经历,心理学专业的学生可能会感兴趣。在用接地发射器制造了一个令人叹为观止的现象后,我一直试图弄明白,对于导入地下的电流,它的真正意义在哪里。这似乎是一项无望的事业,在一年多的时间里,我坚持不懈地工作,但却徒劳无功。这项深奥的研究完全吸引了我,以至于我忘记了其他的一切,甚至忘记了我的安危。最后,当我处于崩溃边缘时,我的身体出于自我保护,陷入了睡眠。当我恢复意识后,我惊慌地发现,我只能记得儿时刚能记事时候的事了,其他的,我都记不起来了。而且很奇怪,那时的场景在我的脑海中无比清晰,这也给我带来一丝宽慰。夜复一夜,在休息的时候,我就开始回想,越来越多的过往经历开始浮现。在缓缓展开的每一幕场景中,母亲始终是主角,我也越来越渴望能想起更多与她相关的事。这种感觉与日俱增,到最后,我决定放弃一切工作,专心恢复记忆。但我发现,要

of my previous existence was revealed. The image of my mother was always the principal figure in the spectacle that slowly unfolded, and a consuming desire to see her again gradually took possession of me. This feeling grew so strong that I resolved to drop all work and satisfy my longing. But I found it too hard to break away from the laboratory, and several months elapsed during which I had succeeded in reviving all the impressions of my past life up to the spring of 1892. In the next picture that came out of the mist of oblivion, I saw myself at the Hotel de la Paix in Paris just coming to from one of my peculiar sleeping spells, which had been caused by prolonged exertion of the brain. Imagine the pain and distress I felt when it flashed upon my mind that a dispatch was handed to me at that very moment bearing the sad news that my mother was dying. I remembered how I made the long journey home without an hour of rest and how she passed away after weeks of agony! It was especially remarkable that during all this period of partially obliterated memory I was fully alive to everything touching on the subject of my research. I could recall the smallest details and the least significant observations in my experiments and even recite pages of text and complex mathematical formulae.

My belief is firm in a law of compensation. The true rewards are ever in proportion to the labor and sacrifices made. This is one of the reasons why I feel certain that of all my inventions, the Magnifying

第六章 遥控力学的艺术
VI. The Art of Telautomatics

离开实验室太难了,几个月过去了,在这期间我成功地恢复了1892年春天之前我的所有记忆。而在遗落记忆的迷雾中,我看到的下一个场景,是在巴黎的和平饭店,由于用脑过度,我刚从一次昏睡中醒来。就在那一刻,我收到了一份急件,上面写着我母亲病危的噩耗,想象一下,当我的脑海中闪过这样一幅画面时,我的悲痛之情简直难以言喻。我想起了我是如何长途跋涉、马不停蹄地赶回了家,想起了母亲是如何遭受了数周的痛苦,然后离开了人世!特别值得一提的是,在这段被遗忘的记忆中,我对涉及我研究课题的一切事情都记忆犹新,我可以回忆起实验中最细微的细节和最微不足道的数据,甚至可以背诵几页纸的内容和复杂的数学公式。

我坚信付出就会有回报。真正的回报永远与付出的劳动和牺牲成正比。这也是我坚信,在我所有的发明中,放大发射器对后世最为重要、最有价值的原因。我之所以这样预测,不是

Transmitter will prove most important and valuable to future generations. I am prompted to this prediction not so much by thoughts of the commercial and industrial revolution which it will surely bring about, but of the humanitarian consequences of the many achievements it makes possible. Considerations of mere utility weigh little in the balance against the higher benefits of civilization. We are confronted with portentous problems which can not be solved just by providing for our material existence, however abundantly. On the contrary, progress in this direction is fraught with hazards and perils not less menacing than those born from want and suffering. If we were to release the energy of atoms or discover some other way of developing cheap and unlimited power at any point of the globe this accomplishment, instead of being a blessing, might bring disaster to mankind in giving rise to dissension and anarchy which would ultimately result in the enthronement of the hated regime of force. The greatest good will comes from technical improvements tending to unification and harmony, and my wireless transmitter is preeminently such. By its means the human voice and likeness will be reproduced everywhere and factories driven thousands of miles from waterfalls furnishing the power; aerial machines will be propelled around the earth without a stop and the sun's energy controlled to create lakes and rivers for motive purposes and transformation of arid deserts into fertile land. Its introduction for

因为它一定会给商业和工业带来翻天覆地的革命，而是因为它会给人类进步带来无限可能。在人类文明这个更高利益面前，单纯的功能效用不足一提。我们面临着不可预知的问题，这些问题不能仅仅通过改善我们的物质生活来解决。相反，在这个方向上的进步充满了危险，其威胁性不亚于那些由物质匮乏和苦难导致的危险。如果我们解锁了原子能，或者找到了在全球任何地方开发廉价和无限能源的新方法，这一成就非但不是一件好事，反而可能会给人类带来灾难，因为它引起了纷争和无政府状态，最终会导致令人厌恶的武力政权上台。技术的进步，唯有以促进和谐与团结为目的，才能带来最大的好处，我的无线发射器正是如此。有了它，人类的声音和图像可以在各地重现，瀑布可以为数千英里外的工厂提供动力，航空机器可以不间断地环绕地球飞行，太阳能可以用来创建湖泊和河流，干旱的沙漠可以变为肥沃的土地。在电报、电话和类似用途中，它的问世可以自动消除静电和所有其他干扰，要知道，这些干扰目前严重限制了无线技术的应用。

telegraphic, telephonic and similar uses will automatically cut out the statics and all other interferences which at present impose narrow limits to the application of the wireless.

This is a timely topic on which a few words might not be amiss. During the past decade a number of people have arrogantly claimed that they had succeeded in doing away with this impediment. I have carefully examined all of the arrangements described and tested most of them long before they were publicly disclosed, but the finding was uniformly negative. A recent official statement from the U.S. Navy may, perhaps, have taught some beguilable news editors how to appraise these announcments at their real worth. As a rule the attempts are based on theories so fallacious that whenever they come to my notice I can not help thinking in a lighter vein. Quite recently a new discovery was heralded, with a deafening flourish of trumpets, but it proved another case of a mountain bringing forth a mouse.

This reminds me of an exciting incident which took place years ago when I was conducting my experiments with currents of high frequency. Steve Brodie had just jumped off the Brooklyn Bridge. The feat has been vulgarized since by imitators, but the first report electrified New York. I was very impressionable then and frequently spoke of the daring printer. On a hot afternoon I felt the necessity of refreshing myself and

第六章 遥控力学的艺术
VI. The Art of Telautomatics

　　这个话题很适时，在这里唠叨几句也无妨。在过去的十年里，一些人傲慢地声称他们已经成功地消除了这些干扰。我仔细研究了他们描述的所有实验，并在他们公布自己的发现之前，对其中的大部分进行了测试，但结论无一例外都是不行。美国海军最近的一份官方声明或许已经教会了一些满嘴谎话的新闻编辑如何评估这些发明成果的真正价值。通常情况下，这些尝试都是基于十分荒谬的理论，所以每次我看到了，都会一笑了之。就在不久前，又有人宣布了一个新发明，引来震耳欲聋的欢呼声，但事实证明，又是雷声大雨点小，一场闹剧而已。

　　这让我想起多年前发生的一件趣事，当时我正在进行高频电流的实验。那阵子史蒂夫·布罗迪刚刚从布鲁克林大桥上跳下，这一壮举后来被模仿者庸俗化了，但第一篇报道却震惊了纽约。我当时还是一个很情绪化的人，经常谈到这个大胆的印刷工。在一个炎热的下午，我想放松一下，于是走进了这座伟大城市中随处可见的酒吧中的一家，那里供应爽口的含12度酒

stepped into one of the popular thirty thousand institutions of this great city where a delicious twelve per cent beverage was served which can now be had only by making a trip to the poor and devastated countries of Europe. The attendance was large and not overdistinguished and a matter was discussed which gave me an admirable opening for the careless remark: "This is what I said when I jumped off the bridge." No sooner had I uttered these words than I felt like the companion of Timotheus in the poem of Schiller. In an instant there was a pandemonium and a dozen voices cried: "It is Brodie!" I threw a quarter on the counter and bolted for the door but the crowd was at my heels with yells: "Stop, Steve!" which must have been misunderstood for many persons tried to hold me up as I ran frantically for my haven of refuge. By darting around corners I fortunately managed—through the medium of a fire-escape—to reach the laboratory where I threw off my coat, camouflaged myself as a hard-working blacksmith, and started the forge. But these precautions proved unnecessary; I had eluded my pursuers. For many years afterward, at night, when imagination turns into spectres the trifling troubles of the day, I often thought, as I tossed on the bed, what my fate would have been had that mob caught me and found out that I was not Steve Brodie!

Now the engineer, who lately gave an account before a technical body of a novel remedy against statics based on a "heretofore unknown

第六章 遥控力学的艺术
VI. The Art of Telautomatics

精的饮料，不过现在只有去贫穷、混乱的欧洲国家才能喝到了。酒吧里人很多，看上去都很普通，大家在讨论一个问题，我忍不住随口插了一句："这正是我跳下桥时说的话。"话音刚落，我感觉自己一下子成了万众焦点。瞬间，现场一阵骚动，十几个人同时喊道："是布罗迪！"我赶紧朝柜台扔了25美分，向门外跑去，人群在我身后大喊："站住，史蒂夫！"我的这句话一定是被误解了，我拼命地想跑回自己的避难所，但好多人想拦住我。我左冲右突，转过几个街角，幸运地从消防通道到达了实验室。我脱下外套，把自己伪装成一个正在打铁的铁匠。不过后来证实，这些其实不必要，我已经成功甩掉了那些追我的人。许多年以后，夜深人静时，白天的琐碎日常像幽灵一样浮现在我的脑海里，有时候，我躺在床上辗转反侧，就会想，那天如果那群人抓住了我，发现我不是史蒂夫·布罗迪，我的命运会是怎样的呢？！

最近，有位工程师在一家技术机构作报告，说自己基于一个"至今不为人知的自然法则"，发明了一种新型抗静电方法。

law of nature", seems to have been as reckless as myself when he contended that these disturbances propagate up and down, while those of a transmitter proceed along the earth. It would mean that a condenser, as this globe, with its gaseous envelope, could be charged and discharged in a manner quite contrary to the fundamental teachings propounded in every elemental text-book of physics. Such a supposition would have been condemned as erroneous, even in Franklin's time, for the facts bearing on this were then well known and the identity between atmospheric electricity and that developed by machines was fully established. Obviously, natural and artificial disturbances propagate through the earth and the air in exactly the same way, and both set up electromotive forces in the horizontal, as well as vertical, sense. Interference can not be overcome by any such methods as were proposed. The truth is this: in the air the potential increases at the rate of about fifty volts per foot of elevation, owing to which there may be a difference of pressure amounting to twenty, or even forty thousand volts between the upper and lower ends of the antenna. The masses of the charged atmosphere are constantly in motion and give up electricity to the conductor, not continuously but rather disruptively, this producing a grinding noise in a sensitive telephonic receiver. The higher the terminal and the greater the space encompassed by the wires, the more pronounced is the effect, but it must be understood that it is purely local

第六章 遥控力学的艺术
Ⅵ. The Art of Telautomatics

这家伙，似乎和我一样鲁莽，他认为静电干扰是纵向传播的，而发射器的电流是沿着地球表面水平传播的。这意味着像地球这样一个被大气包裹的电容器，其充电和放电的方式与每本物理学教科书中提出的基本教义完全相反。这样的假设，即使在富兰克林时代，也会被认为是错误的。众所周知，大气层中的电流和机器产生的电流是完全一样的。很显然，自然电流和人造电流的干扰也以完全相同的方式在地面和空中传播，并且在水平和垂直两个方向上都产生了电动势。电磁干扰不可能通过提出的任何此类方法来克服。事实是这样的：在空气中，每升高一英尺，电势就会增加约50伏，所以，一根天线的顶端和末端之间可能存在着高达2万至4万伏的压力差。带电的大气团不断运动，并向导体释放能量，但这种释放不是连续的，具有干扰性，这在灵敏的电话接收器中就会产生摩擦噪声。终端越高，电线覆盖的面积越大，噪声就越明显，但我们必须明白，这只是局部的问题，真正的麻烦还在后面。

and has little to do with the real trouble.

In 1900, while perfecting my wireless system, one form of apparatus comprised four antennae. These were carefully calibrated to the same frequency and connected in multiple with the object of magnifying the action, in receiving from any direction. When I desired to ascertain the origin of the transmitted impulses, each diagonally situated pair was put in series with a primary coil energizing the detector circuit. In the former case the sound was loud in the telephone; in the latter it ceased, as expected, the two antennae neutralizing each other, but the true statics manifested themselves in both instances and I had to devise special preventives embodying different principles.

By employing receivers connected to two points of the ground, as suggested by me long ago, this trouble caused by the charged air, which is very serious in the structures as now built, is nullified and besides, the liability of all kinds of interference is reduced to about one-half, because of the directional character of the circuit. This was perfectly self-evident, but came as a revelation to some simple-minded wireless folks whose experience was confined to forms of apparatus that could have been improved with an axe, and they have been disposing of the bear's skin before killing him. If it were true that strays performed such antics, it would be easy to get rid of them by receiving without aerials.

第六章 遥控力学的艺术
VI. The Art of Telautomatics

1900 年,我对自己的无线系统——一个有四根天线的设备,做了一些改良。我把天线仔细地校准到相同的频率,然后并联起来,确保从任何方向接收到的信号都可以被放大。而当我想确定脉冲发射的来源时,就将对角的每一对天线串联,用一个初级线圈给检测回路充电。在前一种情况下,电话里的噪声很大;在后一种情况下,噪声消失了,正如预期的那样,两根天线能够互相中和,但是,静电在这两种情况下都真实存在,我必须另辟蹊径,想出基于不同原理的预防措施。

我很早以前就建议过,使用连接到地面两点的接收器可以消除这个由带电空气引发的问题,这个问题在现有的设备中很令人头疼。此外,由于电路的方向性,各种干扰也会减少大约一半。这个道理其实很简单,不言自明,但对一些头脑简单的无线电从业者来说,不亚于启示录。他们的经验还停留在那些用把斧头就可以改良的设备上,而且做事毛躁,急功近利。如果真的是天线导致了干扰,那么解决方案很简单,不用天线接收信号即可。按照这种观点,埋在地下的电线,应该是绝对绝缘的,但事实上,却比裸露在空气中的电线更容易受到某些外部脉冲的影响。客观地说,我们已经取得了一点进展,但不是

But, as a matter of fact, a wire buried in the ground which, conforming to this view, should be absolutely immune, is more susceptible to certain extraneous impulses than one placed vertically in the air. To state it fairly, a slight progress has been made, but not by virtue of any particular method or device. It was achieved simply by discarding the enormous structures, which are bad enough for transmission but wholly unsuitable for reception, and adopting a more appropriate type of receiver. As I pointed out in a previous article, to dispose of this difficulty for good, a radical change must be made in the system, and the sooner this is done the better.

It would be calamitous, indeed, if at this time when the art is in its infancy and the vast majority, not excepting even experts, have no conception of its ultimate possibilities, a measure would be rushed through the legislature making it a government monopoly. This was proposed a few weeks ago by Secretary Daniels, and no doubt that distinguished official has made his appeal to the Senate and House of Representatives with sincere conviction. But universal evidence unmistakably shows that the best results are always obtained in healthful commercial competition. There are, however, exceptional reasons why wireless should be given the fullest freedom of development. In the first place it offers prospects immeasurably greater and more vital to betterment of human life than any other invention or

第六章 遥控力学的艺术
VI. The Art of Telautomatics

靠什么特殊的方法或装置，而仅仅是因为弃用了体积庞大的设备，这些设备对传输信号来说已经够糟了，在接收信号方面也完全不合适，得采用更合适的接收器。正如我在之前文章中指出的那样，要想彻底解决这一难题，必须对系统进行大刀阔斧的改造，而且，事不宜迟。

事实上，这门技术还处于萌芽阶段，绝大多数人，甚至包括专家，对它的最终用途都还没有明确的概念，如果立法机构就此匆忙通过一项法案，使之为政府所垄断，那后果将是灾难性的。几周前，丹尼尔斯部长就提出了这样的倡议。毫无疑问，这位杰出的官员已信誓旦旦地向参议院和众议院提出了议案，但无数事实告诉我们，只有在健康的商业竞争中才能获得最好的结果。而且，对于无线电技术，要给予最充分的研发自由还有特别的理由。首先，与人类历史上的任何其他发明或发现相比，它为改善人类生活提供了不可估量的前景；其次，我们必须认识到，这门技术是在这里得到了全面的发展，要比电话、白炽灯或飞机更有理由被称为"美国"技术。而锐意进取的媒体人和股票经纪人在传播虚假信息方面太出色了，就连《科学

discovery in the history of man. Then again, it must be understood that this wonderful art has been, in its entirety, evolved here and can be called "American" with more right and propriety than the telephone, the incandescent lamp or the aeroplane. Enterprising press agents and stock jobbers have been so successful in spreading misinformation that even so excellent a periodical as the SCIENTIFIC AMERICAN accords the chief credit to a foreign country. The Germans, of course, gave us the Hertz-waves and the Russian, English, French and Italian experts were quick in using them for signaling purposes. It was an obvious application of the new agent and accomplished with the old classical and unimproved induction coil—scarcely anything more than another kind of heliography. The radius of transmission was very limited, the results attained of little value, and the Hertz oscillations, as a means for conveying intelligence, could have been advantageously replaced by sound-waves, which I advocated in 1891. Moreover, all of these attempts were made three years after the basic principles of the wireless system, which is universally employed to-day, and its potent instrumentalities had been clearly described and developed in America. No trace of those Hertzian appliances and methods remains today. We have proceeded in the very opposite direction and what has been done is the product of the brains and efforts of citizens of this country. The fundamental patents have expired and the

第六章 遥控力学的艺术
VI. The Art of Telautomatics

美国人》这样优秀的期刊也将主要的功劳归给了外国。当然,是德国人发现了赫兹波,俄罗斯、英国、法国和意大利的专家很快就将其用于信号传递。不过,这是新媒介的一种常见应用,而且还是用古老的、未经改进的感应线圈来完成的——本质上跟反光通信差不多,传播半径非常有限,所取得的结果也没什么价值,而且赫兹振荡作为一种传递信号的手段,完全可以用我在 1891 年提倡的声波来代替,后者会更有优势。另外,早在做出这些尝试的三年前,无线系统的基本原理及其主要的用途在美国已经得到了明确的描述和研究。今天,那些基于赫兹的设备和方法已不复存在,我们朝着完全相反的方向发展,一切都是这个国家的公民智慧和努力的结晶。基础专利时效已经过期,应用机会向所有人开放。部长的论点主要是出于信号干扰考虑,根据他 7 月 29 日在《纽约先驱报》上的报告,来自强大电台的信号可以在世界上任何一个村庄被拦截。而这一事实,已在我 1900 年的实验中被证明,所以,在美国采取任何限制措施都是白费功夫。

opportunities are open to all. The chief argument of the Secretary is based on interference. According to his statement, reported in the NEW YORK HERALD of July 29th, signals from a powerful station can be intercepted in every village of the world. In view of this fact, which was demonstrated in my experiments of 1900, it would be of little use to impose restrictions in the United States.

As throwing light on this point, I may mention that only recently an odd looking gentleman called on me with the object of enlisting my services in the construction of world transmitters in some distant land. "We have no money," he said, "but carloads of solid gold and we will give you a liberal amount." I told him that I wanted to see first what will be done with my inventions in America, and this ended the interview. But I am satisfied that some dark forces are at work, and as time goes on the maintenance of continuous communication will be rendered more difficult. The only remedy is a system immune against interruption. It has been perfected, it exists, and all that is necessary is to put it in operation.

The terrible conflict is still uppermost in the minds and perhaps the greatest importance will be attached to the Magnifying Transmitter as a machine for attack and defense, more particularly in connection with Telautomatics. This invention is a logical outcome of observations

第六章 遥控力学的艺术
VI. The Art of Telautomatics

为了阐明这一点,我可以提一下,就在最近,一位长相怪异的绅士拜访了我,想请我到某个遥远的地方建造放大发射器。"我们没有钱,"他说,"但有成车装的黄金,我们会给你一笔不菲的费用。"我告诉他,我想先看看我的发明在美国会有什么样的效果,这次谈话就这么结束了。但是我很开心,知道一些未知的干扰因素正在起作用,随着时间的推移,维持不间断通信将变得越来越困难。唯一的补救办法是建立一个不受干扰的系统。这个系统得到过完善,而且已经问世,现在需要做的就是将它投入使用。

可怕的战争冲突仍然是人类最大的顾忌,也许最重要的是将放大发射器作为一种进攻和防御的机器,特别是在遥控力学方面。这项发明,始于我年少时代的观察,并贯穿我的一生,最终才得以问世。当第一批成果发表后,《电气评论》发表社论

begun in my boyhood and continued throughout my life. When the first results were published the ELECTRICAL REVIEW stated editorially that it would become one of the "most potent factors in the advance and civilization of mankind". The time is not distant when this prediction will be fulfilled. In 1898 and 1900 it was offered to the Government and might have been adopted were I one of those who would go to Alexander's shepherd when they want a favor from Alexander. At that time I really thought that it would abolish war, because of its unlimited destructiveness and exclusion of the personal element of combat. But while I have not lost faith in its potentialities, my views have changed since.

War can not be avoided until the physical cause for its recurrence is removed and this, in the last analysis, is the vast extent of the planet on which we live. Only through annihilation of distance in every respect, as the conveyance of intelligence, transport of passengers and supplies and transmission of energy will conditions be brought about some day, insuring permanency of friendly relations. What we now want most is closer contact and better understanding between individuals and communities all over the earth, and the elimination of that fanatic devotion to exalted ideals of national egoism and pride which is always prone to plunge the world into primeval barbarism and strife. No league or parliamentary act of any kind will ever prevent such a calamity.

第六章 遥控力学的艺术
VI. The Art of Telautomatics

称,这将成为"推动人类文明进步的有利因素之一"。这个预言在不久的将来就会实现。在1898年和1900年,我将这个发明呈报给了政府,如果我精于人情世故,或许早就被政府采纳了。当时我真的认为这样就能消除战争,因为它具有无限的破坏性,而且解放了战争中的人力。尽管我对它的潜力充满信心,但我的观点却从那时起发生了变化。

战争是无法避免的,除非消除导致战争不断爆发的物理原因,归根结底,是因为我们生活的这个星球太广阔了。只有在各个方面消除距离,比如信息的传递、乘客和物资的运送以及能源的传输,才有可能创造条件确保永久的和睦关系。我们现在最希望看到的,是全球各地的个人和民族之间交流更密切,彼此更包容,然后消除对民族利己主义和民族自豪感的狂热追求,因为这种狂热追求很容易使世界陷入原始的野蛮纷争。没有哪一个联盟或议会法案可以阻止这样的灾难发生。这些只不过是将弱者置于强者摆布之下的新体制罢了。这个观点,我早在14年前就清楚表达过,当时,安德鲁·卡内基(现已离世)主张将几个主要政府联合起来,成立一个类似于"神圣联盟"

These are only new devices for putting the weak at the mercy of the strong. I have expressed myself in this regard fourteen years ago, when a combination of a few leading governments—a sort of Holy Alliance—was advocated by the late Andrew Carnegie, who may be fairly considered as the father of this idea, having given to it more publicity and impetus than anybody else prior to the efforts of the President. While it can not be denied that such a pact might be of material advantage to some less fortunate peoples, it can not attain the chief object sought. Peace can only come as a natural consequence of universal enlightenment and merging of races, and we are still far from this blissful realization.

As I view the world of today, in the light of the gigantic struggle we have witnessed, I am filled with conviction that the interests of humanity would be best served if the United States remained true to its traditions and kept out of "entangling alliances". Situated as it is, geographically, remote from the theaters of impending conflicts, without incentive to territorial aggrandizement, with inexhaustible resources and immense population thoroughly imbued with the spirit of liberty and right, this country is placed in a unique and privileged position. It is thus able to exert, independently, its colossal strength and moral force to the benefit of all, more judiciously and effectively, than as member of a league.

第六章 遥控力学的艺术
VI. The Art of Telautomatics

的机构。这个想法,得到了美国总统的大力推动,而且在此之前,卡内基对这种想法的宣传和推动就超过了任何人,完全可以被认为是这一想法的创始人。虽然不能否认,这样的契约可能会给一些弱势群体带来物质上的帮助,但并不可能实现我们所追求的主要目标。和平只能作为普遍启蒙和种族融合的自然结果,而我们离这种幸福目标的实现还很遥远。

纵观今日之大千世界,回顾昨日之种种纷争,我深信,如果美国能忠于其传统,不缔结各种关系错综复杂的联盟,人类的利益才能得到最好的保障。从地理位置来看,美国远离各种一触即发的战场,也没有领土扩张的必要,拥有取之不尽的资源和崇尚自由与正义精神的庞大人口,这个国家的地位不可谓不得天独厚。因此,它可以独立地发挥其巨大的实力及道德的力量,要比作为一个联盟的成员,能更明智、更有效地造福全人类。

In one of these biographical sketches, published in the ELECTRICAL EXPERIMENTER, I have dwelt on the circumstances of my early life and told of an affliction which compelled me to unremitting exercise of imagination and self-observation. This mental activity, at first involuntary under the pressure of illness and suffering, gradually became second nature and led me finally to recognize that I was but an automaton devoid of free will in thought and action and merely responsive to the forces of the environment. Our bodies are of such complexity of structure, the motions we perform are so numerous and involved, and the external impressions on our sense organs to such a degree delicate and elusive that it is hard for the average person to grasp this fact. And yet nothing is more convincing to the trained investigator than the mechanistic theory of life which had been, in a measure, understood and propounded by Descartes three hundred years ago. But in his time many important functions of our organism were unknown and, especially with respect to the nature of light and the construction and operation of the eye, philosophers were in the dark.

In recent years the progress of scientific research in these fields has been such as to leave no room for a doubt in regard to this view on which many works have been published. One of its ablest and most eloquent exponents is, perhaps, Felix Le Dantec, formerly assistant of Pasteur. Prof. Jacques Loeb has performed remarkable experiments

第六章 遥控力学的艺术
VI. The Art of Telautomatics

在《电气实验者》上发表的这些文章中,我曾详述了我早年生活的情况,并讲述了在痛苦的折磨下不得不坚持连续想象和自省的经历。这种心理活动,起初是在疾病和痛苦的压力下无意识地进行的,后来逐渐成为我的第二天性,并最终使我认识到,我不过是一台在思想和行动上缺乏自由意志的机器,只是对环境的影响做出反应。我们的身体结构如此复杂,我们所做的动作如此多而繁杂,我们的感官对外界事物的印象如此微妙,难以捉摸,以至于一般人很难理解这一事实。然而,对于训练有素的研究者来说,没有什么比 300 年前笛卡儿在一定程度上理解并提出的生命机械论更令人信服的了。但在他的时代,我们机体的许多重要功能都是未知的,特别是关于光的本质和眼睛的构造与运动方面,哲学家们都还在黑暗之中摸索。

近年来,这些领域的科学研究取得了很大进展,许多关于生命机械论的著作已经出版,人们对这一观点不存在什么质疑。其中最有能力和最有口才的倡导者之一是菲利克斯·勒·丹泰

in heliotropism, clearly establishing the controlling power of light in lower forms of organisms, and his latest book, "Forced Movements", is revelatory. But while men of science accept this theory simply as any other that is recognized, to me it is a truth which I hourly demonstrate by every act and thought of mine. The consciousness of the external impression prompting me to any kind of exertion, physical or mental, is ever present in my mind. Only on very rare occasions, when I was in a state of exceptional concentration, have I found difficulty in locating the original impulses.

The by far greater number of human beings are never aware of what is passing around and within them, and millions fall victims of disease and die prematurely just on this account. The commonest every-day occurrences appear to them mysterious and inexplicable. One may feel a sudden wave of sadness and rake his brain for an explanation when he might have noticed that it was caused by a cloud cutting off the rays of the sun. He may see the image of a friend dear to him under conditions which he construes as very peculiar, when only shortly before he has passed him in the street or seen his photograph somewhere. When he loses a collar button he fusses and swears for an hour, being unable to visualize his previous actions and locate the object directly. Deficient observation is merely a form of ignorance and responsible for the many morbid notions and foolish ideas prevailing.

第六章 遥控力学的艺术
VI. The Art of Telautomatics

克,他曾是巴斯德①的助手。雅克·勒布教授在趋光性方面进行了出色的实验,清楚地确立了低等生物对光的控制能力,他的最新著作《受迫运动》十分具有启示性。这一理论,与其他任何已知的理论一样,得到了科研工作者的认可,但对我来说,它不仅是一个理论,它就是真理,是我每时每刻用行为和思想来证明的真理。对外界事物的印象促使我做出某种行为,无论是身体上还是精神上的,这种印象一直存在于我的脑海中,只有在极少数的情况下,比方说当我处于特别专注的状态下,才发现很难找到最初的冲动。

太多的人从来不关注他们周围和内心世界发生了什么,也正是因为这点,数百万人因患病过早地死去。最普通的日常事件在他们看来都是神秘而且无法解释的。有人可能会突然感到一阵悲伤,并绞尽脑汁寻找一个理由,而他没注意到这是由于云层遮挡了太阳的光线造成的;有人可能会因为在某些非常特殊的情况下看到他好朋友的身影而感到怪异,但原因也许是不久前在街上与这个朋友擦肩而过或在某个地方看到了他的照片;有人可能会因为丢了一枚衣领纽扣而大惊小怪地骂上一个小时,却无法回想起刚刚做了什么事,然后直接找到纽扣。缺乏观察力是无知的一种形式,是许多病态观念和愚昧思想盛行的原因。每十个人中顶多只有一个人不相信心灵感应和其他超自然现象,

---

① 路易斯·巴斯德,法国微生物学家、化学家。

There is not more than one out of every ten persons who does not believe in telepathy and other psychic manifestations, spiritualism and communion with the dead, and who would refuse to listen to willing or unwilling deceivers.

Just to illustrate how deeply rooted this tendency has become even among the clearheaded American population, I may mention a comical incident. Shortly before the war, when the exhibition of my turbines in this city elicited widespread comment in the technical papers, I anticipated that there would be a scramble among manufacturers to get hold of the invention, and I had particular designs on that man from Detroit who has an uncanny faculty for accumulating millions. So confident was I that he would turn up some day, that I declared this as certain to my secretary and assistants. Sure enough, one fine morning a body of engineers from the Ford Motor Company presented themselves with the request of discussing with me an important project. "Didn't I tell you?" I remarked triumphantly to my employees, and one of them said, "You are amazing, Mr. Tesla; everything comes out exactly as you predict." As soon as these hard-headed men were seated I, of course, immediately began to extol the wonderful features of my turbine, when the spokesmen interrupted me and said, "We know all about this, but we are on a special errand. We have formed a psychological society for the investigation of psychic phenomena and we want you to join us in

第六章 遥控力学的艺术
VI. The Art of Telautomatics

不相信唯心论和通灵术，并且拒绝听信有意或无意的谎言。

为了说明这种倾向多么根深蒂固，甚至在头脑清醒的美国人中也是如此，我可以提一件很好笑的事。战前不久，我在这座城市展出了我的涡轮机，引起了各大专业报刊竞相报道，当时我就预料，制造商之间一定会争先恐后地争夺这项发明，特别是那位来自底特律的男人，我对他期望值很高，他有一种不可思议的能力，可以积累数百万美元。我非常确信他总有一天会出现，我向我的秘书和助手们郑重地宣布了这一点。果然，在一个晴朗的早晨，福特汽车公司的一群工程师来到这里，要求与我讨论一个重要的项目。"我说什么来着？"我得意扬扬地对我的员工说。其中一个人说："您太了不起了，特斯拉先生，一切都如您所料。"这些精明冷静的人一坐下来，我就立即开始展示涡轮机的奇妙功能，然而，这时他们有人打断我道："我们都知道这些，但这次来，我们是有特殊任务在身。我们成立了一个心理学会，专门研究心理现象，希望您能加入我们的行列。"我想那些工程师永远不会知道，他们差点就被逐出我的办公室了。

this undertaking." I suppose those engineers never knew how near they came to being fired out of my office.

Ever since I was told by some of the greatest men of the time, leaders in science whose names are immortal, that I possess of an unusual mind, I bent all my thinking faculties on the solution of great problems regardless of sacrifice. For many years I endeavored to solve the enigma of death, and watched eagerly for every kind of spiritual indication. But only once in the course of my existence have I had an experience which momentarily impressed me as supernatural. It was at the time of my mother's death. I had become completely exhausted by pain and long vigilance, and one night was carried to a building about two blocks from our home. As I lay helpless there, I thought that if my mother died while I was away from her bedside she would surely give me a sign. Two or three months before I was in London in company with my late friend, Sir William Crookes, when spiritualism was discussed, and I was under the full sway of these thoughts. I might not have paid attention to other men, but was susceptible to his arguments as it was his epochal work on radiant matter, which I had read as a student, that made me embrace the electrical career. I reflected that the conditions for a look into the beyond were most favorable, for my mother was a woman of genius and particularly excelling in the powers of intuition. During the whole night every fiber in my brain was strained

第六章 遥控力学的艺术
VI. The Art of Telautomatics

　　自从我被当时一些伟大的人、名垂千古的科学界领头羊告知,我拥有不同寻常的头脑后,我便开始不顾一切地投身到研究中,以求解决重大问题。许多年来,我一直致力于解开死亡之谜,密切关注着各种精神现象。但在我的一生中,只经历过一次超自然现象,那是在我母亲去世的时候。当时,我长期饱受疼痛和神经衰弱的折磨,疲惫不堪。一天晚上,我被抬到离我们家大约两个街区的一栋楼里。我无助地躺在那里,心想如果母亲去世,而我却不在她的床边,她一定会给我一个信号。两三个月前,我在伦敦与朋友威廉·克鲁克斯爵士(现已去世)在一块,讨论起了唯心论,当时我完全被这些想法左右了。我可能不在意其他人的想法,但却很容易受他的观点影响,因为我在学生时代就读过他写的关于放射物质的划时代著作,正是这些才使我投身于电气领域。我想,现在正是探索超自然力量的最佳时机,因为我的母亲是一位天才女性,尤其在直觉方面很出色。整个晚上,我紧绷着大脑中的每一根神经,焦急期待着,但什么也没有发生,直到清晨,我睡着了。也许是在昏昏沉沉中,我看到了一朵云,载着一些美丽的天使,其中一个深情地注视着我,逐渐呈现出我母亲的模样,这幅景象慢慢地飘过房间,然后消散了,接着我被一阵难以形容的甜美歌声惊醒。在那一瞬间,一种无法用言语表达的预感袭来,我感觉我的母

in expectancy, but nothing happened until early in the morning, when I fell in a sleep, or perhaps a swoon, and saw a cloud carrying angelic figures of marvelous beauty, one of whom gazed upon me lovingly and gradually assumed the features of my mother. The appearance slowly floated across the room and vanished, and I was awakened by an indescribably sweet song of many voices. In that instant a certitude, which no words can express, came upon me that my mother had just died. And that was true. I was unable to understand the tremendous weight of the painful knowledge I received in advance, and wrote a letter to Sir William Crookes while still under the domination of these impressions and in poor bodily health. When I recovered I sought for a long time the external cause of this strange manifestation and, to my great relief, I succeeded after many months of fruitless effort. I had seen the painting of a celebrated artist, representing allegorically one of the seasons in the form of a cloud with a group of angels which seemed to actually float in the air, and this had struck me forcefully. It was exactly the same that appeared in my dream, with the exception of my mother's likeness. The music came from the choir in the church nearby at the early mass of Easter morning, explaining everything satisfactorily in conformity with scientific facts.

This occurred long ago, and I have never had the faintest reason since to change my views on psychical and spiritual phenomena, for

第六章 遥控力学的艺术
VI. The Art of Telautomatics

亲应该刚刚去世了,事实也的确如此。我无法理解这种痛苦的预感的寓意,在百思不得其解、身体每况愈下的情形下,我给威廉·克鲁克斯爵士写了一封信。当我康复后,我花了很长时间来找寻这种奇怪现象的外部原因,令我大为宽慰的是,经过几个月的徒劳无功后,最终我还是成功了。我曾看过一位著名艺术家的画作,他以云彩象征季节,一群天使看上去像飘浮在空中,这幅画面给了我强烈的冲击。除了我母亲的样子,这和我梦中出现的景象一模一样。我听到的歌声是在复活节清晨的弥撒中,从附近教堂的唱诗班传来的,这一切都以科学事实为依据得到了完美的解释。

这是很久以前的事了,从那以后,我再也没有改变过对这些心理和精神现象的看法,在我看来,这些根本就是无稽之谈。

which there is absolutely no foundation. The belief in these is the natural outgrowth of intellectual development. Religious dogmas are no longer accepted in their orthodox meaning, but every individual clings to faith in a supreme power of some kind. We all must have an ideal to govern our conduct and insure contentment, but it is immaterial whether it be one of creed, art, science or anything else, so long as it fulfills the function of a dematerializing force. It is essential to the peaceful existence of humanity as a whole that one common conception should prevail.

While I have failed to obtain any evidence in support of the contentions of psychologists and spiritualists, I have proved to my complete satisfaction the automatism of life, not only through continuous observations of individual actions, but even more conclusively through certain generalizations. These amount to a discovery which I consider of the greatest moment to human society, and on which I shall briefly dwell. I got the first inkling of this astounding truth when I was still a very young man, but for many years I interpreted what I noted simply as coincidences. Namely, whenever either myself or a person to whom I was attached, or a cause to which I was devoted, was hurt by others in a particular way, which might be best popularly characterized as the most unfair imaginable, I experienced a singular and undefinable pain which, for want of a better term, I have

第六章 遥控力学的艺术
VI. The Art of Telautomatics

这种信仰只是智力发展的自然结果。宗教教义不再因其原本的意义被接受，但每个人仍执迷于某种至高无上力量的信仰。我们必须有一个完美典范来指导我们的行为，确保获得满足感，只要这个典范能发挥非物质化力量的作用，至于它是教义、艺术、科学还是其他的什么，并不重要。人类要想和平共处，有一个共同的信仰至关重要。

虽然我未能获得任何证据来支持心理学家和唯心论者的论点，但让我很满意的是，我已经证实了生命的自动属性。这一结论的得出，不仅归功于我对个体行为的持续观察，更有赖于我的归纳总结。这一发现，我认为是人类社会最重要的时刻，对此我将做简要概述。在很小的时候，我就对这个惊人的事实有了初步的了解，但多年来，我一直把我注意到的事情简单地解释为巧合。比方说，每当我自己或与我有关联的人，或我所投身的事业，受到了别人某种特殊方式的伤害，按流行的说法，也就是最不公平的对待时，我就会感到一种特殊的、无法形容的痛苦，由于找不到更好的说法，我把这种痛苦统称为"极痛"，此后不久，那些施加"极痛"的人无一例外地遭遇灾难。在经历了许多次这样的情况之后，我把这些事告诉了一些朋友，他们开始相信我逐渐形成的这套理论的真实性，这个理论可以

qualified as "cosmic", and shortly thereafter, and invariably, those who had inflicted it came to grief. After many such cases I confided this to a number of friends, who had the opportunity to convince themselves of the truth of the theory which I have gradually formulated and which may be stated in the following few words:

Our bodies are of similar construction and exposed to the same external influences. This results in likeness of response and concordance of the general activities on which all our social and other rules and laws are based. We are automata entirely controlled by the forces of the medium being tossed about like corks on the surface of the water, but mistaking the resultant of the impulses from the outside for free will. The movements and other actions we perform are always life preservative and though seemingly quite independent from one another, we are connected by invisible links. So long as the organism is in perfect order it responds accurately to the agents that prompt it, but the moment that there is some derangement in any individual, his self-preservative power is impaired. Everybody understands, of course, that if one becomes deaf, has his eyesight weakened, or his limbs injured, the chances for his continued existence are lessened. But this is also true, and perhaps more so, of certain defects in the brain which deprive the automaton, more or less, of that vital quality and cause it to rush into destruction. A very sensitive and observant being, with his

第六章 遥控力学的艺术
VI. The Art of Telautomatics

用下面的话来概括：

我们的身体结构相似，受到同样的外部影响。这就导致了反应的相似性和一般活动的一致性，我们所有的社会准则和法律规则都是基于此。我们是完全受媒介力量控制的机器人，像水面上的软木塞一样被抛来抛去，误认为自己具有自由意志，不受外部作用的影响。我们的运动和其他行为都是为了生存，虽然看起来彼此完全独立，但我们却被无形的联系连接在一起。只要有机体处于正常状态，它就会对外部刺激做出准确的反应，但一旦任何个体出现某种失调，他的自我保护能力就会受到影响。当然，大家都知道，如果一个人失聪，或视力减弱，或四肢受伤，他继续生存的机会就会减少，大脑中的某些缺陷也是如此，也许更甚，这些缺陷或多或少地剥夺了"这台机器"的生命力，导致它迅速走向毁灭。一个非常敏感和善于观察的人，其机能高度发达并且完好无损，能够顺应环境条件的变化精确行动，被赋予了一种超自然的感知能力，使他能够避开难以察觉的微妙危险。当他与那些控制器官有严重缺陷的人接触时，这种感觉就会显现出来，他会感到"极痛"。这一点已经在数百个例子中得到证实，我正在邀请其他研究自然科学的学者关注

highly developed mechanism all intact, and acting with precision in obedience to the changing conditions of the environment, is endowed with a transcending mechanical sense, enabling him to evade perils too subtle to be directly perceived. When he comes in contact with others whose controlling organs are radically faulty, that sense asserts itself and he feels the "cosmic" pain. The truth of this has been borne out in hundreds of instances and I am inviting other students of nature to devote attention to this subject, believing that through combined and systematic effort results of incalculable value to the world will be attained.

The idea of constructing an automaton, to bear out my theory, presented itself to me early but I did not begin active work until 1893, when I started my wireless investigations. During the succeeding two or three years a number of automatic mechanisms, to be actuated from a distance, were constructed by me and exhibited to visitors in my laboratory. In 1896, however, I designed a complete machine capable of a multitude of operations, but the consummation of my labors was delayed until late in 1897. This machine was illustrated and described in my article in the CENTURY MAGAZINE of June, 1900, and other periodicals of that time and, when first shown in the beginning of 1898, it created a sensation such as no other invention of mine has ever produced. In November, 1898, a basic patent on the novel art

第六章 遥控力学的艺术
Ⅵ. The Art of Telautomatics

这个问题，相信通过共同的、系统的努力，将为世界带来不可估量的价值。

我很早就有构建一个自动机的想法，用以证明我的理论，但直到1893年我开始无线电研究后才正式投入这项工作。在随后的两三年里，我建造了一些可以远程遥控的自动装置，并在我的实验室里向参观者展示。1896年，我设计了一台能够进行多种操作的机器，然而，直到1897年年底才彻底完成。我在1900年6月的《世纪杂志》和当时其他期刊上发表的文章中对这台机器进行了说明和描述，当它在1898年初首次展出时，引起了我其他发明从未有过的轰动。1898年11月，我获得了这项新技术的基本专利，我所公布的东西似乎令人难以置信，首席审查员来到纽约亲眼见证后才授予我专利。我记得，后来我去华盛顿拜访一位官员，想将这项发明提供给美国政府，当我告诉他我所取得的成就时，他突然大笑起来。当时没有人认为

was granted to me, but only after the Examiner-in-Chief had come to New York and witnessed the performance, for what I claimed seemed unbelievable. I remember that when later I called on an official in Washington, with a view of offering the invention to the Government, he burst out in laughter upon my telling him what I had accomplished. Nobody thought then that there was the faintest prospect of perfecting such a device. It is unfortunate that in this patent, following the advice of my attorneys, I indicated the control as being effected through the medium of a single circuit and a well-known form of detector, for the reason that I had not yet secured protection on my methods and apparatus for individualization. As a matter of fact, my boats were controlled through the joint action of several circuits and interference of every kind was excluded. Most generally I employed receiving circuits in the form of loops, including condensers, because the discharges of my high-tension transmitter ionized the air in the hall so that even a very small aerial would draw electricity from the surrounding atmosphere for hours. Just to give an idea, I found, for instance, that a bulb 12″ in diameter, highly exhausted, and with one single terminal to which a short wire was attached, would deliver well on to one thousand successive flashes before all charge of the air in the laboratory was neutralized. The loop form of receiver was not sensitive to such a disturbance and it is curious to note that it is becoming popular at this

第六章 遥控力学的艺术
VI. The Art of Telautomatics

改进这样一个装置有什么前景。不幸的是，在这项专利中，我根据律师的建议只指出，控制是通过一个单一电路和一个众所周知的探测器来实现的，因为那时候，我还没有为我的个性化方法和装置申请专利保护。但事实上，我的装置是通过几个电路的共同作用来控制的，各种干扰都被排除在外。大多数情况下，包括电容器，我采用的都是环路接收电路，因为我的高压发射器放电会使大厅里的空气离子化，所以即使是一截非常小的天线也会从周围的大气中吸取电能，持续几个小时。举个例子，我发现，一个直径12英寸的灯泡，高度放电，通过单一的终端与一根短导线相连，在实验室的所有空气的电荷被中和之前，能够连续闪烁1000多次。环路电路接收器对这种干扰并不敏感，但奇怪的是，到这么晚它才开始流行起来。实际上，它接收的能量比天线或长接地线要少得多，但它恰好消除了目前无线设备所固有的一些缺陷。在观众面前展示我的发明时，参观者会提出各种问题，无论多么复杂，远程机器人都会用手势回答他们。这在当时被认为是神奇的，但其实非常简单，因为是我自己通过这个装置在回答问题。

late date. In reality it collects much less energy than the aerials or a long grounded wire, but it so happens that it does away with a number of defects inherent to the present wireless devices. In demonstrating my invention before audiences, the visitors were requested to ask any questions, however involved, and the automaton would answer them by signs. This was considered magic at that time but was extremely simple, for it was myself who gave the replies by means of the device.

At the same period another larger telautomatic boat was constructed, a photograph of which is shown in this number of the ELECTRICAL EXPERIMENTER. It was controlled by loops, having several turns placed in the hull, which was made entirely water-tight and capable of submergence. The apparatus was similar to that used in the first with the exception of certain special features I introduced as, for example, incandescent lamps which afforded a visible evidence of the proper functioning of the machine.

These automata, controlled within the range of vision of the operator, were, however, the first and rather crude steps in the evolution of the Art of Telautomatics as I had conceived it. The next logical improvement was its application to automatic mechanisms beyond the limits of vision and at great distance from the center of control, and I have ever since advocated their employment as instruments of

第六章 遥控力学的艺术
VI. The Art of Telautomatics

在同一时期,我还建造了另一艘更大的远程遥控船,其照片展示在这一期的《电气实验者》中。这艘船是由线圈控制的,船体上缠绕了几圈电线,电线完全防水,能够浸入水中。这个装置与第一台很相似,但我增加了一些特殊功能,例如,我安装了白炽灯,这样,机器的运转情况就一目了然。

正如我所设想的那样,这些在操作者视线范围内控制的自动装置,是远程自动化技术发展的第一步,也是相当粗糙的一步。下一个合乎逻辑的改进是将其应用于视野范围之外和远离控制中心的自动装置,从那时起,我就主张将其设计成一种武器,以代替枪支。媒体对我公布的成果评价很随意,他们认为这些成就很特别,但没有什么新颖性,虽然它的重要性目前似

warfare in preference to guns. The importance of this now seems to be recognized, if I am to judge from casual announcements through the press of achievements which are said to be extraordinary but contain no merit of novelty, whatever. In an imperfect manner it is practicable, with the existing wireless plants, to launch an aeroplane, have it follow a certain approximate course, and perform some operation at a distance of many hundreds of miles. A machine of this kind can also be mechanically controlled in several ways and I have no doubt that it may prove of some usefulness in war. But there are, to my best knowledge, no instrumentalities in existence today with which such an object could be accomplished in a precise manner. I have devoted years of study to this matter and have evolved means, making such and greater wonders easily realizable.

As stated on a previous occasion, when I was a student at college I conceived a flying machine quite unlike the present ones. The underlying principle was sound but could not be carried into practice for want of a prime-mover of sufficiently great activity. In recent years I have successfully solved this problem and am now planning aerial machines devoid of sustaining planes, ailerons, propellers and other external attachments, which will be capable of immense speeds and are very likely to furnish powerful arguments for peace in the near future. Such a machine, sustained and propelled entirely by reaction, is shown

第六章 遥控力学的艺术
VI. The Art of Telautomatics

乎已经得到了认可。不管怎样，利用现有的无线设备，以一种不太成熟的方式发射一架飞机，让它沿着某种既定的航线飞行，并在几百英里外执行某些任务，这些都是切实可行的。这种机器也可以通过多种方式进行机械控制，毫无疑问它在战争中可能会有一定的用处。但据我所知，目前还没有任何装置可以精确地完成这样的任务。我花了多年的时间来研究这个问题，并想到了一些方法，来实现这种以及更高级的目标。

如上所述，当我还是一名大学生的时候，我就设想了一种与现在完全不同的飞行器，其基本原理是合理的，但由于缺乏一个足够强大的原动机而无法付诸实践。近年来，我已经成功地解决了这个问题，目前正在设计没有机翼、副翼、螺旋桨和其他外部附件的飞行器，它们将具有极快的速度，并且很可能在不久的将来为人类和平提供巨大的支撑。这种完全靠反作用力维持和推进的机器有机械和无线两种控制模式。通过安装相应的设备，就可以将导弹发射到空中，投放到数千英里之外任何指定的地点。但我们不会止步于此。遥控力学最终将被创造

on page 108 and is supposed to be controlled either mechanically or by wireless energy. By installing proper plants it will be practicable to project a missile of this kind into the air and drop it almost on the very spot designated, which may be thousands of miles away. But we are not going to stop at this. Telautomata will be ultimately produced, capable of acting as if possessed of their own intelligence, and their advent will create a revolution. As early as 1898 I proposed to representatives of a large manufacturing concern the construction and public exhibition of an automobile carriage which, left to itself, would perform a great variety of operations involving something akin to judgment. But my proposal was deemed chimerical at that time and nothing came from it.

At present many of the ablest minds are trying to devise expedients for preventing a repetition of the awful conflict which is only theoretically ended and the duration and main issues of which I have correctly predicted in an article printed in the SUN of December 20, 1914. The proposed League is not a remedy but on the contrary, in the opinion of a number of competent men, may bring about results just the opposite. It is particularly regrettable that a punitive policy was adopted in framing the terms of peace, because a few years hence it will be possible for nations to fight without armies, ships or guns, by weapons far more terrible, to the destructive action and range of which there is virtually no limit. A city, at any distance whatsoever from the

第六章 遥控力学的艺术
VI. The Art of Telautomatics

出来，能够拥有自己的智慧，可以实施各种行动，它们的问世将引发一场革命。早在1898年，我就向一家大型制造企业的代表提议，建造并公开展示一种自动运输装置，它可以自行完成各种涉及自主判断的操作。但我的建议在当时被认为是不切实际的，没有任何后续。

目前，许多有识之士都在设法制定权宜之计，以防止可怕的冲突重演，这场冲突，只是在理论上结束了。我在1914年12月20日的《太阳报》上发表的一篇文章中，正确预测了这场冲突的持续时间和主要问题。组成联盟这个提议并不是一种补救措施，相反，一些有识之士认为，它可能会带来恰恰相反的结果。特别令人遗憾的是，在制定和平条款时采纳了一种惩罚性政策，因为几年后，各国将不再使用军队、船只或枪支作战，而是用更可怕的武器进行战斗，其破坏力和攻击范围几乎没有

enemy, can be destroyed by him and no power on earth can stop him from doing so. If we want to avert an impending calamity and a state of things which may transform this globe into an inferno, we should push the development of flying machines and wireless transmission of energy without an instant's delay and with all the power and resources of the nation.

第六章 遥控力学的艺术
VI. The Art of Telautomatics

任何限制。一座城市，无论离敌人多远，都能被摧毁，而地球上没有任何力量可以阻止这样的事发生。如果我们想避免即将到来的灾难，阻止将地球变为人间炼狱，我们应该毫不迟疑地尽所有力量，集所有资源推动飞行器和无线能量传输的发展。

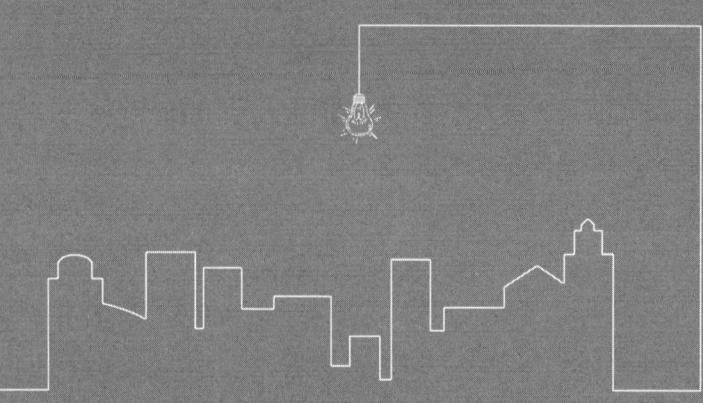

【 The end 】

【完】

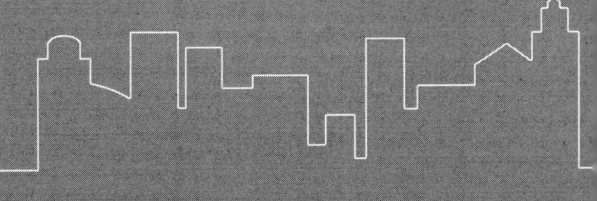

译者后记

翻译《特斯拉自传》，于我而言，颇具挑战。作为旷古烁今的一位发明天才，尼古拉·特斯拉在这本自传中，讲述了自己坎坷而辉煌的发明人生。

他的发明，例如交流电、无线能量传输、世界系统等，任何一项都足以改变我们所处的世界。而我作为一介文科生，虽视翻译为一生挚爱，对于机械及电气原理等相关知识却近乎一窍不通。在翻译本书的过程中，我碰到了大量这方面的术语，让我无从下手，苦不堪言。也许有人说，是我不懂利用翻译技术，网上有专业的术语语料库不知道查阅。的确，现在随着人工智能、语料库等翻译技术的发展，特别是ChatGPT的横空出世，好像翻译已经变成了一件极其简单的事情。而我，似乎是一个因循守旧的人，对翻译的理解还停留在一杯茶、一本字典、一个下午的状态。

在翻译本书的过程中，我首先要感谢安徽工程大学教职工羽毛球协会。因为羽协，我结识了许多学识渊博的球友。我要特别感谢安徽工程大学机械学院的疏达教授、钟相强教授，电气学院的刘世林教授，正是三位球友专业且耐心的指点，我才得以扫清书中所涉的一切术语障碍。

其次，我要感谢湖南知书达礼文化传播有限公司的张总。与张总结识多年，前几年已经有过几次译著的合作，所以双方也算是知根知底，彼此信赖了吧。张总为人豁达，有着在商人身上很少见的侠义之气，欣赏我对翻译的痴迷，在出版发行上也是有商有量。这本《特斯拉自传》最终将以双语对照版的形式出版，也是经双方充分沟通后才确定的。

以双语对照版出版，不仅可供对尼古拉·特斯拉感兴趣的人阅读，更可以作为一本翻译实践案例，供广大翻译专业学生及爱好者对照阅读。我亦深知，译无止境，双语对照版只会让我的翻译不足甚至错误更直观地暴露在广大读者面前，但是，若能以反面教材之形式起到警示作用，谁又敢说这不是一种对翻译的贡献呢？如若有三五处翻译，能让读者拍手称妙，进而加深了对翻译的理解与认识，岂不快哉！

吾爱有二。静时浸淫翻译，动时驰骋羽场，一静一动，相得益彰。唯盼岁月静好，如此日复一日，人生无憾矣！

希望广大读者亦能觅得人生真爱，并持之以恒，身处喧嚣之尘世，寻得内心之安宁！共勉之。

张文明

2024 年 2 月 20 日